Cambridge Essentials

Mathematics

Julie Bolter
Steven Ellis
Susan Timperley

Series editors: Graham Newman
Peter Sherran

Support 9

 **CAMBRIDGE**
UNIVERSITY PRESS

CAMBRIDGE
UNIVERSITY PRESS

University Printing House, Cambridge CB2 8BS, United Kingdom

Cambridge University Press is part of the University of Cambridge.

It furthers the University's mission by disseminating knowledge in the pursuit of education, learning and research at the highest international levels of excellence.

www.cambridge.org
Information on this title: www.cambridge.org/9780521723824

© Cambridge University Press 2010

First published 2010
Reprinted 2013

Printed in Italy by Rotolito Lombarda S.p.A.

A catalogue record for this publication is available from the British Library

ISBN 978-0-521-72382-4 Paperback with CD-ROM for Windows and Mac

Take advantage of the pupil CD

Cambridge Essentials Mathematics comes with a pupil CD in the back. This contains the entire book as an interactive PDF file, which you can read on your computer using free Adobe Reader software from Adobe (www.adobe.com/products/acrobat/readstep2.html). As well as the material you can see in the book, the PDF file gives you extras when you click on the buttons you will see on most pages; see the inside front cover for a brief explanation of these.

To use the CD, simply insert it into the CD or DVD drive of your computer. You will be prompted to install the contents of the CD to your hard drive. Installing will make it easier to use the PDF file, because the installer creates an icon on your desktop that launches the PDF directly. However, it will run just as well straight from the CD.

If you want to install the contents of the disc onto your hard disc yourself, this is easily done. Just open the disc contents in your file manager (for Apple Macs, double click on the CD icon on your desktop; for Windows, open My Computer and double click on your CD drive icon), select all the files and folders and copy them wherever you want.

Take advantage of the teacher CD

The *Teacher Material* CD-ROM for *Cambridge Essentials Mathematics* contains enhanced interactive PDFs. As well as all the features of the pupil PDF, teachers also have access to e-learning materials and links to the *Essentials Mathematics* Planner – a new website with a full lesson planning tool, including worksheets, homeworks, assessment materials and guidance. The e-learning materials are also fully integrated into the Planner, letting you see the animations in context and alongside all the other materials.

Powers of 10

- Reading and writing positive powers of 10
- Multiplying and dividing by powers of 10
- Multiplying and dividing by 0.1 and 0.01
- Ordering decimals
- Using inequality signs $<$ and $>$

Keywords

You should know

explanation 1a   explanation 1b

1 Copy and complete each of these. The first one has been done for you.

  a $10^2 = 10 \times 10 = 100$

  b $10^3 = 10 \times \square \times \square = \square$

  c $10^6 = \underline{\hspace{2cm}} = \square$

  d $10^0 = \square$

  e $10^8 = \underline{\hspace{2cm}} = \square$

  f $10^{10} = \underline{\hspace{2cm}} = \square$

2 Write these numbers using powers.

  a 1000   b 10 000   c 100   d 100 000   e 1

3 Write these numbers using powers of 10.

  a 300   b 900   c 7000   d 50 000

  e 2 000 000   f 400 000   g 800 000   h 60 000 000

4 Write each expression as a number.

  a 5×10^3 b 3×10^2 c 4×10^4 d 7×10^1

  e 9×10^3 f 6×10^0 g 2×10^1 h 15×10^2

  i 28×10^2 j 41×10^3 k 231×10^0 l 76×10^4

explanation 2a   explanation 2b

5 Work out these multiplications without using a calculator.

a 24×100

b 53×1000

c 215×100

d 1000×47

e 2.8×10

f 15.706×10

g 0.43×10

h $72.01 \times 10\,000$

i 0.64×1000

j 0.5×100

k $0.36 \times 10\,000$

l $0.09 \times 10\,000$

6 Work out these divisions without using a calculator.

a $68 \div 10$

b $52 \div 1000$

c $7 \div 100$

d $4.6 \div 10$

e $6.3 \div 100$

f $12.5 \div 100$

g $0.37 \div 10$

h $0.51 \div 100$

i $0.04 \div 100$

j $0.84 \div 1000$

k $0.08 \div 1000$

l $1.04 \div 10\,000$

7 Copy and complete these calculations.

a $53 \times \square = 530$

b $\square \times 1000 = 4400$

c $5.8 \times \square = 580$

d $\square \times 100 = 120$

e $730 \div \square = 7.3$

f $\square \div 100 = 0.45$

g $0.6 \div \square = 0.006$

h $\square \div 1000 = 0.14$

i $145 \div \square = 0.0145$

8 a   Emily has been saving £10 a week and now has £160 saved.

For how many weeks has she been saving?

b   Her goal is to save £380 in total. If she continues saving £10 a week how more many weeks will that take?

9 a   Samir's chocolate cake recipe uses 75 g of butter.

How many grams of butter will he need to make 10 chocolate cakes?

b   Samir knows that there are 1000 g in 1 kg.

How many kilograms of butter will he need for the 10 cakes?

---

explanation 3

10 Which of these is equivalent to 3.4×0.1?

    A 3.4×10 B $3.4 \div 100$ C $3.4 \div 10$ D $3.4 \div 0.1$

11 Which of these is equivalent to 25.9×0.01?

    A $25.9 \div 100$ B 25.9×100 C 25.9×10 D $25.9 \div 0.01$

12 Work these out without using a calculator.
The first two have been started for you.

  a $31 \times 0.1 = 31 \times \dfrac{1}{10} = 31 \div \square = \square$

  b $58 \times 0.01 = 58 \times \dfrac{1}{100} = \square \div \square = \square$

c	14×0.1	d	72×0.01	e	4×0.1	f	93×0.01
g	1.5×0.1	h	7.4×0.1	i	12.4×0.01	j	10.6×0.01
k	25.6×0.1	l	29.4×0.01	m	50.2×0.01	n	214.25×0.1

---

explanation 4

13 Which of these is equivalent to $7.3 \div 0.1$?

    A $7.3 \div 10$ B 7.3×10 C 7.3×0.1 D 7.3×100

14 Which of these is equivalent to $14.6 \div 0.01$?

    A 14.6×10 B $14.6 \div 10$ C $14.6 \div 100$ D 14.6×100

15 Work these out without using a calculator.
The first two have been started for you.

  a $23 \div 0.1 = 23 \div \dfrac{1}{10} = 23 \times \square = \square$

  b $46 \div 0.01 = 46 \div \dfrac{1}{100} = \underline{\hspace{2cm}} = \square$

c	$18 \div 0.1$	d	$43 \div 0.01$	e	$7 \div 0.1$	f	$26 \div 0.01$
g	$3.6 \div 0.1$	h	$8.2 \div 0.1$	i	$31.5 \div 0.01$	j	$70.4 \div 0.01$
k	$203.6 \div 0.1$	l	$0.3 \div 0.1$	m	$0.8 \div 0.01$	n	$0.25 \div 0.1$

16 Match each calculation to its answer.

a

57×0.1
57×0.01
$57 \div 0.1$
$57 \div 0.01$

5700
0.57
5.7
570

b

0.34×0.1
0.34×0.01
$0.34 \div 0.1$
$0.34 \div 0.01$

3.4
0.034
0.0034
34

17 a Jack poured orange juice into four small glasses.
Each glass held 0.1 litres of juice. How much juice did he need?

b How much juice would he need for 15 glasses?

c If he had 2.5 litres of orange juice how many glasses could he fill?

[explanation 5a] [explanation 5b]

18 Put these decimals in ascending order, smallest to biggest.
Use the number line to help you.

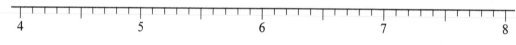

a 5.6, 4.9, 5.3, 4.2   b 7.8, 6.7, 5.4, 5.7   c 4.5, 6.4, 5.6, 6.5, 7.4, 4.7

19 Put these decimals in ascending order. Use the number line to help you.

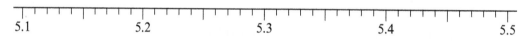

a 5.32, 5.12, 5.41, 5.33   b 5.45, 5.43, 5.47, 5.44   c 5.5, 5.49, 5.39, 5.4

20 Which number in each pair is bigger?
Use the number lines in questions **18** and **19** to help you.

a 5.1 or 4.9   b 7.3 or 7.7   c 5.34 or 5.4   d 5.4 or 5.45

21 Which number in each pair is smaller?

a 2.6 or 2.3   b 15.8 or 15.3   c 23.74 or 23.69

d 20.53 or 20.43   e 0.65 or 0.64   f 50.233 or 50.236

g 2.982 or 2.981   h 0.3256 or 0.3258   i 2.9742 or 2.9751

22 Put these decimals in ascending order.

a   2.15, 2.11, 2.18, 2.2

b   0.25, 0.3, 0.15, 0.19, 0.21

c   5.235, 5.325, 5.24, 5.33, 5.302

d   15.0345, 15.135, 15.045, 15.099

e   0.0067, 0.0103, 0.0092, 0.0011, 0.01

23 Copy and complete these. Use < or > instead of the box.

a   6.7 $\square$ 7.6

b   9.05 $\square$ 9.04

c   23.45 $\square$ 23.54

d   16.53 $\square$ 16.5

e   13.532 $\square$ 13.542

f   0.956 $\square$ 0.965

g   1.0084 $\square$ 1.0078

h   8.8 $\square$ 8.08

i   4.17 $\square$ 4.126

24 Write the numbers in each pair in the correct boxes so that $\square$ < $\square$ is true.

a   5.8, 8.58

b   12.33, 12.3651

c   0.775, 0.768

d   1.0052, 1.0049

25 Write the numbers in each pair in the correct boxes so that $\square$ > $\square$ is true.

a   0.59, 0.54

b   7.008, 7.08

c   560.87, 560.807

d   24.2355, 24.3255

26 Sara weighed some chemistry samples in the science laboratory.
Write her results in order from largest to smallest mass.

7.3871 g   7.8351 g   7.38 g   7.0835 g

27 These are the top five throws in the boys' shot put at the school athletics competition.

Lenny 7.235 m   Uri 7.325 m   Aidan 7.24 m   Jacob 7.33 m   Sam 7.30 m

Put the top five throws in descending order. Who won the competition?

Rounding and estimation

- Rounding numbers to the nearest 100
- Rounding numbers to make estimates
- Rounding decimals to one or two decimal places

Keywords

You should know

explanation 1a　explanation 1b

1　Round each of these numbers to the nearest 10. Use the number line to help you.

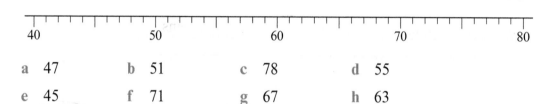

a	47	b	51	c	78	d	55
e	45	f	71	g	67	h	63

2　Round each of these numbers to the nearest 10.
You could draw number lines to help.

a	26	b	5	c	99	d	127	e	547
f	678	g	312	h	202	i	705	j	995

3　Round each of these numbers to the nearest 100. Use the number line to help you.

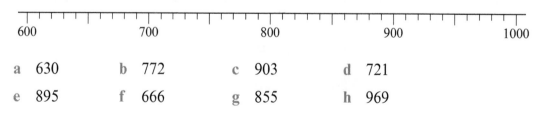

a	630	b	772	c	903	d	721
e	895	f	666	g	855	h	969

4　Round each of these numbers to the nearest 100.
You could draw number lines to help.

a	320	b	578	c	535	d	1243	e	4886
f	6265	g	9899	h	1034	i	8098	j	9999

5 This table shows you the lengths of some rivers.

River	Nile	Amazon	Mississippi	Yangtze	St Lawrence	Rio Grande
Length in kilometres	6484	6516	6019	5797	3058	3034

    a Round each length to the nearest 10 km.

    b Round each length to the nearest 100 km.

    c Which river has the same length when rounded to the nearest 10 km and 100 km?

6 You have 96 528 km of tubing in your arteries and veins.

    a Round this length to the nearest 10 km.

    b Round this length to the nearest 100 km.

7 The circumference of the world is 40 066 km at the equator and 39 992 km through the poles.

    a What are these distances to the nearest 10 km?

    b What are these distances to the nearest 100 km?

8 Mira had some money saved in her bank account.

She told her mother that she had £250 to the nearest £10, and £300 to the nearest £100.

Write down three amounts that Mira might have saved.

(explanation 2)

9 Estimate the answers to these questions by rounding to the nearest 10.
Do not use a calculator. Show your working.

    a 18×8 b 34×7 c $79 \div 9$ d $52 \div 8$

    e 91×9 f 63×11 g $67 \div 13$ h $83 \div 21$

10 Estimate the answers to these questions by rounding to the nearest 10 or 100.

Do not use a calculator. Show your working.

a $98 + 63$ b $102 - 39$ c 106×18 d $113 \div 22$

e 99×29 f $298 \div 47$ g 323×49 h $603 \div 58$

> It may be easier to round one number to the nearest 10 and one to the nearest 100.

11 Estimate the answers to these questions by rounding to the nearest 10 or 100.

Do not use a calculator. Show your working.

a $27 + (9 \times 58)$ b $(47 \times 11) - 148$

c $(19 \times 18) + 114$ d $208 \times 12 \times 8$

e $307 \times (98 \div 8)$ f $892 - (98 \div 13)$

g $\dfrac{19 \times 97}{22}$ h $\dfrac{61 \times 102}{19 \times 8}$

> Remember to use BIDMAS.

12 Screen 1 of the Odeon Cinema has 23 rows of seats with 18 seats per row.

Estimate how many seats there are in Screen 1.

13 On a holiday flight to France the average weight of a suitcase was 22 kg.

There were 152 suitcases on board the aeroplane.

Estimate the total mass of the suitcases.

explanation 3a   explanation 3b   explanation 3c   explanation 3d

14 Round these decimals to the nearest whole number.
You could use a number line or place value to help you.

a   24.2   b   36.8   c   108.5   d   299.7

e   46.36   f   537.84   g   57.52   h   76.09

i   3.426   j   34.085   k   5.602   l   0.579

15 A 7-day bus pass costs £13.70

How much will it cost to buy fourteen 7-day bus passes for students on a school trip?

Use a calculator to find the answer and round it to the nearest £1.

16 Round these numbers to one decimal place.
You could use a number line or place value to help you.

a 4.53   b 15.67   c 5.45   d 32.06

e 0.74   f 25.75   g 16.09   h 7.99

17 Round these numbers to one decimal place.

a 11.585   b 24.844   c 10.9357   d 9.603   e 152.007

f 3.4923   g 0.0616   h 123.0941   i 193.95   j 4.9976

18 Use a calculator to work out the area of each of these rectangles.

Round each answer to one decimal place.

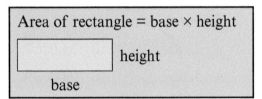

Area of rectangle = base × height

height

base

a

3.52 cm

4.87 cm

b

3.52 cm

4.87 cm

19 Mr Sykes is building a bookcase.

He has a piece of timber 350 cm long to divide into three equal-sized pieces.

Use a calculator to work out how long each piece will be.

Round your answer to the nearest 0.1 cm.

20 A 1.5 kg bag of sweets is shared evenly among 16 children.

What weight of sweets will each child receive, to the nearest 0.1 kg?

You may use a calculator.

21 An empty rucksack weighs 3.68 kg.

How much will 12 of these rucksacks weigh?

Round your answer to one decimal place (1 d.p.). You may use a calculator.

explanation 4a explanation 4b

22 Round these numbers to two decimal places (2 d.p.).
You could use a number line or place value to help you.

a 2.823	b 6.857	c 12.893	d 0.734	e 1.007
f 21.872	g 0.758	h 7.355	i 33.097	j 17.344

23 Round these numbers to 2 d.p.

a 25.8555	b 34.0767	c 0.036 27	d 8.8888
e 5.2271	f 0.006 99	g 0.009 45	h 8.098 24

24 A roll of curtain material contains 24.5 m of fabric.

It is cut into six equal pieces.

Use a calculator to work out the length of each piece.

Round your answer to 2 d.p.

25 Estimate the answers to these by rounding to the nearest whole number.

Do not use a calculator. The first one has been started for you.

a $2.7 \times 9.5 \approx 3 \times 10 = \square$ b $19.7 \div 3.6$ c 5.4×21.1

d $26.8 - 2.88 \times 3.15 + 4.7$ e $\dfrac{12.27 + 5.89}{1.15 + 2.017}$

Remember to use **BIDMAS**.

Directed numbers

- Adding and subtracting positive and negative numbers
- Multiplying and dividing negative numbers

Keywords

You should know

explanation 1a   explanation 1b

1 Find the missing terms in these sequences. Use the number line to help you.

a $-6, -4, -2, \square, \square, \square$

b $-5, -2, 1, \square, \square, \square$

c $4, 1, -2, \square, \square, \square$

d $-7, -5, -3, \square, \square, \square$

e $-4, -6, -8, \square, \square, \square$

f $7, 4, \square, \square, -5, \square$

g $-9, -6, -3, \square, \square, \square$

h $12, 7, \square, \square, -8, \square$

i $-15, -11, -7, \square, \square, \square$

*j $12, 5, \square, \square, -16, \square$

2 Write the calculations shown by these diagrams.

a

b

c

d

e

f

3 Work these out. Use the number line to help you.

a $1 - 8$

b $-3 + 7$

c $-4 - 6$

d $-8 + 6$

e $-5 + 10$

f $-6 + 5$

g $-3 + 7$

h $-6 - 4$

i $-5 + 2 + 3$

j $-9 + 3 + 4$

k $6 - 8 - 3$

l $-11 + 4 + 8$

4 Copy and complete these. Each ☐ stands for a number and each ○ stands for an operation (+ or −).

a $-5 + \square = 3$

b $2 - \square = -4$

c $-3 + \square = 7$

d $-3 \bigcirc \square = -1$

e $-6 \bigcirc \square = 3$

f $-5 \bigcirc \square = -10$

g $3 \bigcirc \square = -7$

h $-6 \bigcirc \square = 1$

i $\square + 9 = 4$

j $\square - 4 = -4$

k $\square + 7 = -4$

l $\square - 6 = -10$

 explanation 2a   explanation 2b

5 James said, '$-3 - +7$ is easy because $+7$ is the same as 7.'

He wrote: $-3 - +7 = -3 - 7$

$$= -10$$

Use this method to work out these calculations.

+7 is just the same as 7.

a $2 - +6$

b $4 + +5$

c $-3 - +3$

d $-4 - +7$

e $8 + +9$

f $0 - +4$

g $-10 + +1$

h $-12 - +13$

6 Copy and complete these number patterns.

a

$3 + 2 = 5$
$3 + 1 = 4$
$3 + 0 = 3$
$3 + -1 = 2$
$3 + -2 = \square$
$3 + -3 = \square$
$3 + -4 = \square$

b

$1 + 2 = 3$
$1 + 1 = 2$
$1 + 0 = \square$
$1 + -1 = \square$
$1 + -2 = \square$
$1 + -3 = \square$
$1 + -4 = \square$

c

$-2 + 4 = 2$
$-2 + 3 = 1$
$-2 + 2 = \square$
$-2 + 1 = \square$
$-2 + 0 = \square$
$-2 + -1 = \square$
$-2 + -2 = \square$

d

$-3 + 2 = -1$
$-3 + 1 = \square$
$-3 + 0 = \square$
$-3 + -1 = \square$
$-3 + -2 = \square$
$-3 + -3 = \square$
$-3 + -4 = \square$

7 Copy and complete these statements.
Use your answers to questions **5** and **6** to help you.

a Adding −2 is the same as …

b Adding −3 is the same as …

c Subtracting +3 is the same as …

d Subtracting +5 is the same as …

e Adding −4 is the same as …

8 Copy and complete these. Each □ stands for a number and each ○ stands for an operation (+ or −).

a 8 + −6

= 8 ○ 6

= □

b 5 − +3

= 5 ○ 3

= □

c −4 + +9

= −4 ○ 9

= □

d 2 − +6

= 2 ○ 6

= □

9 Work these out.

a 3 + −7

b 5 + −5

c −4 + −3

d −1 − +4

e 8 + −9

f 0 − +4

g −10 + −1

h −2 − +3

i −3 + −2

j 5 + −6

k 10 + +5

l 5 − +6

explanation 3

10 Copy and complete these number patterns.

a

3 − 2 = 1
3 − 1 = 2
3 − 0 = 3
3 − −1 = □
3 − −2 = □
3 − −3 = □
3 − −4 = □

b

1 − 3 = −2
1 − 2 = □
1 − 1 = □
1 − 0 = □
1 − −1 = □
1 − −2 = □
1 − −3 = □

c

−2 − 3 = −5
−2 − 2 = □
−2 − 1 = □
−2 − 0 = □
−2 − −1 = □
−2 − −2 = □
−2 − −3 = □

d

−3 − 1 = −4
−3 − 0 = □
−3 − −1 = □
−3 − −2 = □
−3 − −3 = □
−3 − −4 = □
−3 − −5 = □

11 Copy and complete these statements.
Use your answers to questions **6** and **10** to help you.

   a Subtracting −2 is the same as …   b Subtracting −3 is the same as …

   c Adding −5 is the same as …   d Subtracting −10 is the same as …

   e Adding −10 is the same as …

12 Copy and complete these.

   a 8 + −6   b 5 − +3   c −4 + +9   d 2 − +6

      = 8 ◯ 6   = 5 ◯ 3   = −4 ◯ 9   = 2 ◯ 6

      = ☐   = ☐   = ☐   = ☐

   e 3 − −8   f 4 − +5   g 3 + −8   h 1 − −9

      = 3 ◯ 8   = 4 ◯ 5   = 3 ◯ 8   = 1 ◯ 9

      = ☐   = ☐   = ☐   = ☐

13 Work these out.

   a 3 − −7   b 6 + −3   c 5 − −3   d −8 − −4

   e 2 − −9   f 5 − +2   g −6 + −6   h −5 − −3

   i −1 + −7   j −7 − −6   k 4 + −5   l 8 − +6

14 Work these out.

   a −4 − −9   b −8 − +6   c −2 + −1   d −6 − −3

   e 3 − −4   f 1 − +5   g −4 + −3   h −6 − −2

   i −3 + −6   j −5 − −7   k 7 + −2   l 10 − +7

15 This is a magic square.

In a magic square each row, column and diagonal has
the same total. This total is called the magic number.

−3	4	−4
−2		
	−6	

   a How do you know that the magic number for this
magic square is −3?

   b How do you know that the centre number is −1?

   c Copy and complete the magic square.

16 Here are some magic squares. Copy and complete each magic square so that its rows, columns and diagonals have the same total.

a

−1		
4	2	0
	−2	

Magic number = 6

b

−6	8	−2
4		
		6

Magic number = ☐

c

	3	−2
1	−1	
	−5	

Magic number = ☐

d

2	0	−7	9
	5		−2
	6		
−3		6	

Magic number = 4

e

7			−6
		−1	4
−2	3		
0		6	−5

Magic number = ☐

*17 Copy and complete these addition pyramids. To find the number in each brick, add the numbers in the two bricks below it.

a

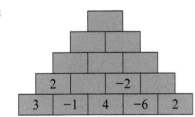

b

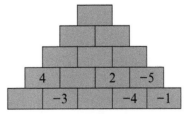

c

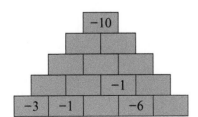

d

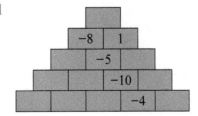

15

explanation 4

18 Copy and complete these number patterns.

a
```
2 × 2 = 4
2 × 1 = 2
2 × 0 = 0
2 × −1 = ☐
2 × −2 = ☐
2 × −3 = ☐
2 × −4 = ☐
```

b
```
4 × 3 = 12
4 × 2 = ☐
4 × 1 = ☐
4 × 0 = ☐
4 × −1 = ☐
4 × −2 = ☐
4 × −3 = ☐
```

c
```
5 × 3 = 15
5 × 2 = ☐
5 × 1 = ☐
5 × 0 = ☐
5 × −1 = ☐
5 × −2 = ☐
5 × −3 = ☐
```

19 Describe each of the following statements as 'true' or 'false'.
Where a statement is false, write the correct answer to the calculation.

a $3 \times -5 = -15$ b $4 \times -4 = 0$ c $-4 \times 3 = 12$

d $-1 \times 4 = -3$ e $3 \times -2 = -6$ f $-2 \times 3 = 1$

20 Work these out.

a 3×-7 b 5×-3 c -6×6 d -7×4

e 8×9 f 0×-4 g -10×6 h -2×8

i -12×2 j 5×-4 k -10×5 l 5×-6

explanation 5a   explanation 5b

21 Copy and complete these number patterns.

a
```
−2 × 2 = −4
−2 × 1 = −2
−2 × 0 = 0
−2 × −1 = ☐
−2 × −2 = ☐
−2 × −3 = ☐
−2 × −4 = ☐
```

b
```
−4 × 3 = −12
−4 × 2 = ☐
−4 × 1 = ☐
−4 × 0 = ☐
−4 × −1 = ☐
−4 × −2 = ☐
−4 × −3 = ☐
```

c
```
−5 × 3 = −15
−5 × 2 = ☐
−5 × 1 = ☐
−5 × 0 = ☐
−5 × −1 = ☐
−5 × −2 = ☐
−5 × −3 = ☐
```

22 Copy and complete this multiplication grid.

×	−3	−2	−1	0	1	2	3
3	−9				3		
2							6
1							
0		0					
−1					−2		
−2		4		0			
−3							

23 Copy the sentences. Use the words 'positive' or 'negative' to complete them.

a When you multiply a positive number by a negative number, the answer is …

b When you multiply a negative number by a positive number, the answer is …

c When you multiply a negative number by a negative number, the answer is …

d When you multiply a positive number by a positive number, the answer is …

24 Describe each of the following statements as 'true' or 'false'.
Where a statement is false, write the correct answer to the calculation.

a $-4 \times -5 = -20$ b $-6 \times -4 = 24$ c $-4 \times -4 = 0$

d $-2 \times 4 = 8$ e $-2 \times -2 = -4$ f $5 \times -2 = -10$

g $-3 \times 3 = -9$ h $-3 \times -2 = 5$ i $-6 \times 0 = -6$

25 Work these out.

a -4×-7 b 6×-2 c -5×-6 d -8×4

e -8×-3 f 20×-2 g -10×-7 h -3×6

i -12×6 j -5×-8 k -2×15 l 0×-6

m 3×-1 n 8×-5 o -7×-7 p -6×9

q 15×-4 r 0×-8 s -12×4 t -7×-8

*26 Copy and complete this multiplication grid.

×		3		−5	
		−12			
−3			−6		
	−16				12
				−25	−30
	80				

27 Use each multiplication calculation to complete the equivalent division calculations.

The first one has been done for you.

a $−2 \times 8 = −16$ i $−16 \div 8 = −2$ ii $−16 \div −2 = 8$

b $−10 \times −5 = 50$ i $50 \div −5 = \Box$ ii $50 \div −10 = \Box$

c $−8 \times 6 = −48$ i $−48 \div −8 = \Box$ ii $−48 \div 6 = \Box$

d $30 \times −2 = −60$ i $−60 \div 30 = \Box$ ii $−60 \div −2 = \Box$

28 Copy the sentences. Use the words 'positive' or 'negative' to complete them.

a When you divide a positive number by a negative number, the answer is …

b When you divide a negative number by a positive number, the answer is …

c When you divide a negative number by a negative number, the answer is …

29 Work these out.

a $−35 \div −7$ b $6 \div −2$ c $−7 \times −8$ d $−8 \div 4$

e $−7 \times −6$ f $50 \div −5$ g $−12 \times −3$ h $−5 \times 9$

i $−12 \div 4$ j $−5 \times −8$ k $−30 \div 5$ l $40 \div −5$

m $3 \div −1$ n $7 \times −5$ o $−8 \div −8$ p $−27 \div 9$

q $−1 \times −4$ r $0 \div −3$ s $−25 \times 4$ t $−16 \div −4$

Expressions

- Identifying the correct order for a calculation
- Writing expressions
- Substituting into expressions

Keywords

You should know

explanation 1a   explanation 1b

1 Match each calculation to its value. The first one has been done for you.

a $18 - 4 \times 3$ Answer: **G**

b $24 + 12 \div 2$

c $2 + 3^2$

d $12 \div 3 \times 2$

e $6^2 \div 2$

f $(8 - 3)^2$

g $15 - 5 \times 3$

A 30

B 11

C 18

D 8

E 0

F 25

G 6

2 Each calculation has been worked out incorrectly!
Find the mistakes and write out the correct solutions.

a
```
12 × 3 – 50
= 36 – 50
= 14
```

b
```
20 – 10 + 4
= 20 – 14
= 6
```

c
```
24 – 10 × 2
= 20 – 24
= –4
```

d
```
20 × 10 + 2
= 20 × 12
= 240
```

e
```
2 × 10²
= 20²
= 400
```

f
```
5 + 5²
= 10²
= 100
```

3 Work out these calculations.

a $5 + 4 \times 2$		**b** $2 \times (4 + 5)$		**c** $18 - 3 + 4$	
d $5 + 4^2$		**e** $12 - (5 + 2)$		**f** $36 \div 3 \times 2$	
g $(4 + 5)^2$		**h** $12 - 2^3$		**i** $14 \div (10 - 3)$	
j $12 - 6 \div 3$		**k** $15 + 24 \div 4$		**l** $(8 - 3) \times 6$	
m $(3 \times 4)^2$		**n** 3×4^2		**o** $12 - 8 + 4$	
p $12 - (8 + 4)$		**q** $24 \div (4 \times 2)$		**r** $24 \div 4 \times 2$	

explanation 2

4 Each calculation has been worked out incorrectly!
Find the mistakes and write out the correct solutions.

a
$$\frac{20}{4} + 8$$
$$= 28 \div 4$$
$$= 7$$

b
$50 - 10 \times 4 + 3$
$= 40 \times 4 + 3$
$= 160 + 3$
$= 163$

c
$$\frac{6 + 4}{2}$$
$$= 3 + 4$$
$$= 7$$

d
$2 \times 4 - 3 \times 2$
$= 8 - 3 \times 2$
$= 5 \times 2$
$= 10$

e
$2 + 3 \times 10^2$
$= 5 \times 100$
$= 500$

f
$2 \times 5 + 5 \times 2$
$= (10 + 5) \times 2$
$= 30$

5 Work out these calculations.

a $5 + 4 \div 2$	**b** $12 \div (4 + 2)$	**c** $20 - 12 \div 4$	
d $16 \div 2 + 6$	**e** $15 - 10 \div 5$	**f** $36 \div 3 - 2$	
g $\dfrac{20}{2} + 4$	**h** $\dfrac{20 + 4}{2}$	**i** $8 + \dfrac{24}{4}$	
j $\dfrac{8 + 24}{4}$	**k** $\dfrac{12 + 8}{5}$	**l** $\dfrac{20}{7 + 3}$	
m $6 + \dfrac{14}{2}$	**n** $\dfrac{36}{4} - 8$	**o** $\dfrac{18}{9 - 6}$	

6 Work out these calculations.

a $2 \times 3 + 4 \times 5$

b $2 \times (4 + 2) \times 5$

c $4 + 6 \times 2 + 5$

d $23 - 4 \times 5 + 2$

e $12 + 7 - 3 + 6$

f $12 + 5 \times 6 \div 2$

g $\dfrac{20 - 8}{7 - 4}$

h $12 + \dfrac{20}{5} - 7$

i $3 \times 5 - \dfrac{18}{2}$

j $18 + 3 \times 2 + 6$

k $20 - 4 \times 3 + 5$

l $8 \times 4 - 12 \div 2$

m $\dfrac{16 - 4}{2 + 1}$

n $18 - \dfrac{23 - 7}{8}$

o $3 + 2 \times \dfrac{15}{3}$

---

explanation 3

---

7 Jennifer was asked to work out $3 \times 4 + 5 \times 2$.

She wrote on the board $(3 \times 4) + (5 \times 2) = 22$.

Her teacher said that the calculation was right but that it did not need brackets.

Explain why the brackets are not needed.

*8 Which of these calculations do not need brackets?

a $(4 + 6) \times 2 = 20$

b $28 - (5^2) = 3$

c $18 - (2 \times 4) = 10$

d $15 - (13 - 8) = 10$

e $(27 + 3) - 4 = 26$

f $(4 + 3)^2 = 49$

g $4^2 - (5 \times 3) = 1$

h $(6 - 2)^2 + 8 = 24$

i $8 - (15 - 7) = 0$

j $18 - (4 \times 3) + 6 = 12$

k $(12 \times 3) - (4 \times 5) = 16$

l $8 - 12 \div (2 + 4) = 6$

*9 Put brackets in these calculations, *where necessary*, to make them correct.

a $15 - 4 \times 3 = 33$

b $8 \times 4 + 6 = 80$

c $6 + 5 \times 4 = 26$

d $3 + 5^2 = 64$

e $10 - 7 + 9 = 12$

f $32 \div 4 \times 2 = 4$

g $36 \div 3^2 = 4$

h $24 + 8 \div 2 = 16$

i $8 - 3^2 = 25$

j $25 - 6 \times 4 = 1$

k $2 \times 10^2 = 200$

l $8 + 4 \times 2 + 1 = 36$

explanation 4a   explanation 4b

10 Match the expressions with the statements.
The first one has been done for you.

a   The number x doubled   Answer: **D**

b   One more than the number x

c   The number x multiplied by itself

d   Three more than the number x

e   The number x added to a different number, y

f   The number x multiplied by 3

g   Two less than the number x

A $x - 2$

B $x + y$

C $3x$

D $2x$

E $x + 1$

F x^2

G $3 + x$

11 Write an expression for each of these sets of instructions.

a   Start with y and add 1 to it.

b   Start with y and multiply it by 2.

c   Start with y and subtract 5 from it.

d   Start with y and divide it by 2.

e   Start with y and subtract it from 10.

f   Start with y and square it.

g   Start with y and add it to 4.

h   Start with y and divide 10 by it.

*12 Match the expressions with the statements.
The first one has been done for you.

a   3 more than double the number p Answer: **B**

b   Double the number that is 3 more than p

c   The number p doubled, then added to a different number, q

d   The number p added to a different number, q,
then multiplied by 2

e   The number p added to double the number q

f   3 more than the square of the number p

g   3 added to a number p and then squared

h   The number p squared and added to a different number, q

A $2(p + q)$

B $2p + 3$

C $p^2 + q$

D $(p + 3)^2$

E $2(p + 3)$

F $p^2 + 3$

G $p + 2q$

H $2p + q$

*13 Write a statement, starting with x, to describe each expression.

a $2x + 1$ b $2(x + 1)$ c $x^2 + 1$

d $2(x - 3)$ e $2x - 3$ f $\dfrac{x}{2} + 4$

g $\dfrac{x + 4}{2}$ h $3(x - 2)$ i $\dfrac{x - 2}{3}$

---

explanation 5

14 Find the value of each expression when $x = 4$.

a $x + 3$ b $2x$ c $3x$

d $3x - 2$ e $3(x - 2)$ f $4x - 3$

g $4(x - 3)$ h $12 - x$ i $18 - 2x$

j $\dfrac{x}{2} + 3$ k $\dfrac{x + 3}{2}$ l $\dfrac{60}{x + 1}$

*15 Find the value of each expression in question 14 when $x = -2$.

16 Find the value of each expression when $x = 6$.

a $5(x + 2)$ b $5x + 2$ c $6x - 3$

d $6(x - 3)$ e $2(3x - 7)$ f $7 - 3x$

*g $\dfrac{5x - 6}{2}$ *h $\dfrac{3x + 2}{4}$ *i $\dfrac{3x}{2} - 8$

*17 Find the value of each expression in question 16 when $x = -2$.

*18 Find the value of each expression in question 16 when $x = -4$.

19 Find the value of each expression when $x = 5$ and $y = 6$.

a $x + y$ b $x - y$ c $2x + y$

d $x + 3y$ e $2x - 3y$ f $20 - x - y$

g $8 - (x - y)$ h $\dfrac{x - 1}{2}$ i $\dfrac{x + 1}{y}$

*20 Find the value of each expression in question 19 when $x = -3$ and $y = 2$.

Simplifying expressions

- Simplifying expressions by collecting like terms
- Simplifying expressions involving brackets
- Simplifying expressions involving products

Keywords

You should know

explanation 1

1 These cards show expressions.

a Sort the cards into matching pairs to find the two odd cards out.

| A | 3x | B | 4x | C | 3x + 1 + 3x − 1 | D | x + x + x |

| E | x + 6 | F | x + 1 + x + 1 | G | 2x + 2 | H | 2x + 2x |

| I | 6x | J | 3 + x | K | 3 + x + 3 | L | 2x + 1 |

b Write expressions which match the two cards left over.

2 Simplify these expressions.

a	x + x	b	x + x + 1	c	1 + x + x + 3
d	x + 3 + x + 2	e	3x + 2x + x	f	4x + 3 + x
g	x + 4x + 5x	h	x + 4x + 5	i	2x + 1 + 5x
j	x + 2 + 4x + 3	k	2x + 5 + 6x + 8	l	9x + 7 + 6x + 5
m	x + y + y	n	2x + 2y + 3x	o	x + 3y + 2x + 5y
p	2x + 3 + y + 4	q	3x + y + 2y + 5x + 3	r	2x + 6y + 1 + x + 3y
s	2x + 8y + 6x + 3	t	2x + 3y + 4 + y + 6	u	6y + 2 + 3x + y + 1

explanation 2

3 Work these out.

a $8 - 5 + 7$

b $-4 + 6 - 2$

c $-6 - 5 - 3$

d $-5 + 8 - 1$

e $3 - 12 + 4$

f $-1 - 7 + 4$

g $-6 + 3 + 2$

h $-7 - 6 + 5$

i $-5 + 4 - 2$

j $-8 + 6 - 5$

k $-3 + 8 - 2$

l $5 - 3 - 4$

4 Simplify these expressions.

a $x - 5 + 2$

b $x + x - 1$

c $2x + 1 - x$

d $2x + 8 - 5$

e $5x + 13 - 7$

f $4 + 7x - 4$

g $6x - 2x + 3$

h $3x - 5 - 2x$

i $4x - 3 - 2$

j $3 + x - 4$

k $1 + 2x - 4$

l $3x - 4 - 3$

m $4 + 3x - 4$

n $5x + 3 + 7x$

o $2x - 3 + 2x$

5 Simplify these expressions.

a $1 - 2x + 4 + 3x$

b $x + 4 + x - 6$

c $2x + 5 - x + 3$

d $2x + 3 - x + 3 - x$

e $5x + 3 - x - 7$

f $4 - 2x - 4 + 7x$

g $9x - 4 - 2x + 3$

h $6x + 5 + 2x - 3$

i $4x - 3 - 4x - 3$

j $3 - 2x + 4 + 5x$

k $1 + 7x - 4 - 5x$

l $3x + 4 - x - 2$

6 Simplify these expressions.

a $2x + 5y - x - 3$

b $x + 4 - y - 6$

c $2x - 4y - 2y + 3x$

d $2x + 3 - x + 3 - y$

e $5x - 3 - 4x + 4$

f $6x + 5 - 2y - 3$

g $3y - 2x - 4 + 5x$

h $3x + 4y - 5x - 3y$

i $6 - 3x + y + 4x$

j $5 - 5x - 3 + 4y + 3$

k $5x - 3 - 2y + 6 - 8x$

l $8 + 5x - 3y - 2y - 9$

m $7x - 2y + 6 - 4x + 3 - 5y$

n $8 - 5x - 4y + 6x - 3y$

o $5y - 7x + 4y - 5x - 6$

p $3x - 4y - 5 + x - 2y - 8$

7 In these algebra caterpillars, the expression in each section is the sum of the expressions in the previous two sections.

Calculate the missing expressions. Give your answers in their simplest form.

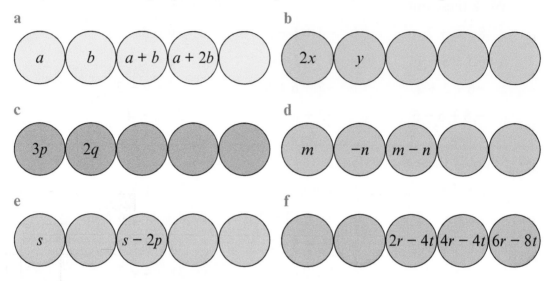

a

| a | b | $a + b$ | $a + 2b$ | |

b

| $2x$ | y | | | |

c

| $3p$ | $2q$ | | | |

d

| m | $-n$ | $m - n$ | | |

e

| s | | $s - 2p$ | | |

f

| | | $2r - 4t$ | $4r - 4t$ | $6r - 8t$ |

8 Each card shows an algebraic expression.

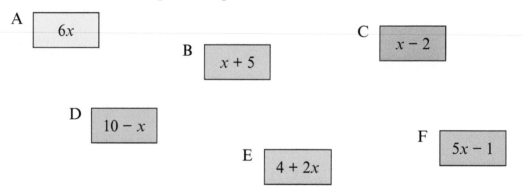

A $6x$

B $x + 5$

C $x - 2$

D $10 - x$

E $4 + 2x$

F $5x - 1$

a Choose two of the cards that have a total of $8x + 4$.

b Choose two of the cards that have a total of $6x + 4$.

c Choose two of the cards that have a total of 15.

d Choose two cards that have a mean of $4x + 2$.

e What is the total of all the expressions on the cards?

explanation 3

9 In these algebra pyramids, the expression in each brick is the total of the
   expressions in the two bricks beneath it. Copy and complete the pyramids.
   Give each answer in its simplest form.

a
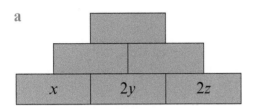

b
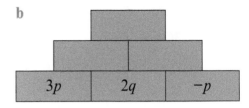

c
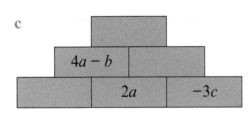

d
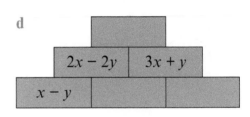

e
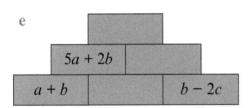

f
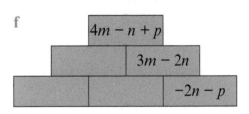

explanation 4a   explanation 4b   explanation 4c

10 Simplify these expressions. The first one has been done for you.

   a $2 \times p = 2p$

   b $3 \times q$

   c $t \times 7$

   d $2r \times 3$

   e $3n \times -4$

   f $10 \times -k$

   g $-2 \times q$

   h $-5 \times 2q$

   i $-2b \times -3$

27

11 Match each bracket with its expansion.

The first one has been done for you.

a $2(4x - 1)$ Answer: **B**

A $8x - 12$

b $6(x - 2)$

B $8x - 2$

c $4(2x + 1)$

C $4x + 6$

d $3(3x - 2)$

D $6x - 12$

e $2(2x + 3)$

E $9x - 6$

f $4(2x - 3)$

F $6x + 12$

g $3(2x + 4)$

G $8x + 4$

12 Expand the brackets in these expressions.

a $3(x + 8)$ b $4(n - 2)$ c $7(t + 1)$

d $10(h + 3)$ e $12(p + 2)$ f $5(b - 2)$

g $8(x - 4)$ h $3(2n + 1)$ i $2(5 - 2t)$

j $5(4x + 3)$ k $2(5n - 3)$ l $6(2t - 3)$

*13 Expand the brackets in these expressions.

a $-5(x + 2)$ b $-2(n + 5)$ c $3(5 - 3t)$

d $6(2x - 4)$ e $-(h + 3)$ f $-5(b - 2)$

g $-3(p - 2)$ h $-2(5 - t)$ i $3(4 - 3x)$

j $-(2t - 3)$ k $-2(3n + 1)$ l $-6(5 - 2x)$

> explanation 5

14 Work these out.

a Expand $3(x + 2)$.

b Expand $4(x + 1)$.

c Show that $3(x + 2) + 4(x + 1) = 7x + 10$.

15 Expand the brackets and then simplify.

a $5(x + 1) + 4(x + 5)$ b $2(d + 1) + 6(d + 5)$ c $3(k + 4) + 2(k + 2)$

d $4(n + 3) + 5(n + 1)$ e $6(x + 3) + 5(x + 2)$ f $4(b + 1) + 3(b + 2)$

g $5(p − 1) + 4(p + 3)$ h $4(x − 5) + 2(x + 5)$ i $5(n − 1) + 3(n + 2)$

*16 Work these out.

a   i Expand $4(3x − 2)$.

 ii Expand $−2(x − 1)$.

 iii Show that $4(3x − 2) − 2(x − 1) = 10x − 6$.

b   i Expand $2(5x − 1)$.

 ii Expand $−(x − 4)$.

 iii Show that $2(5x − 1) − (x − 4) = 9x + 2$.

*17 Expand the brackets and then simplify.

a $3(x − 1) + 2(x − 5)$ b $7(d − 1) − 3(d + 5)$ c $5(k + 4) − 8(k − 2)$

d $9(b + 1) − 5(b + 2)$ e $2(x − 5) + 3(x − 5)$ f $4(n − 1) − 6(n − 2)$

explanation 6a	explanation 6b	explanation 6c

18 Simplify these products.

a $4 \times p$ b $3 \times 5q$ c $4 \times 7t$

d $8r \times 3$ e $9n \times 4$ f $10k \times 3$

g $p \times q$ h $a \times 2b$ i $4m \times n$

j $3a \times 2b$ k $5a \times −2b$ l $−3n \times −6p$

m $2b \times c \times 3$ n $3p \times 2q \times 5$ o $4 \times m \times 2n \times 6$

*19 Expand the brackets in these expressions.

a $a(b + 2)$ b $−c(f + 5)$ c $g(5 − 3f)$

d $6(2x − 4y)$ e $a(b + c)$ f $5c(b − 2)$

g $−3(p − 2q)$ h $2s(5 − 4t)$ i $y(4 − 3x)$

29

explanation 7 ▭▭▭▭▭▭▭▭▭▭▭▭▭▭▭▭▭▭

*20 Simplify these expressions.

a $t \times t$ b $k \times k \times k$ c $m \times m \times m \times m$

d $3 \times f \times f$ e $g \times g \times 6$ f $p \times 4 \times p$

g $q \times q \times q \times 2$ h $3 \times b \times b \times b \times b$ i $2 \times d \times d \times 3$

j $5 \times p \times 2 \times p$ k $3 \times s \times 2 \times s \times 4$ l $r \times r \times 4 \times r \times 6$

*21 Simplify these expressions.

a $p \times p$ b $2p \times p$ c $p \times 3p$

d $3p \times 2p$ e $5p \times 3p$ f $2p \times -3p$

g $p \times p \times p$ h $3p \times p \times p$ i $2p \times 3p \times p$

*22 Simplify these expressions.

a $p \times q$ b $4t \times u$ c $h \times 2h$

d $5f \times 3g$ e $4h \times 3h$ f $6j \times 2j$

g $p \times q \times q$ h $p \times p \times q \times q \times q$ i $3b \times b \times c$

j $2k \times 4k \times l$ k $5 \times n \times 6 \times m \times m$ l $4h \times h \times 3h$

*23 Copy and complete the table. The first row has been done for you.

Terms	Sum of the terms	Product of the terms
a, a	$2a$	a^2
$a, 3$		
a, b		
$a, b, 4$		
$a, a, 3$		
$2a, b$		
$2a, a$		
$2a, 3a$		
$2a, 3a, 4$		

Angles

- Using the angle rules to solve problems
- Identifying alternate and corresponding angles
- Solving angle problems involving parallel lines

Keywords

You should know

explanation 1a   explanation 1b

1 Look at each diagram.

Work out the size of each angle marked with a letter.

State which angle rule you use.

a
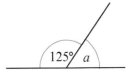
125° a

b
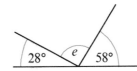
b
63°

c
253°
c

d
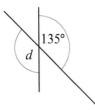
135°
d

e

28° e 58°

f

140°
f

g
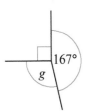
167°
g

h
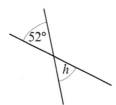
52°
h

i
63°
i

j
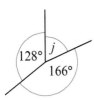
128° j
166°

k
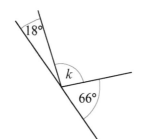
18°
k
66°

l
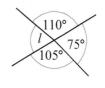
110°
l 75°
105°

explanation 2a | explanation 2b

2 Look at each triangle. Work out the size of each angle marked with a letter.

a
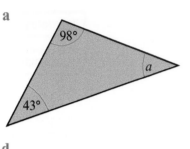

b
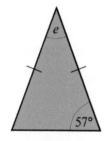

c
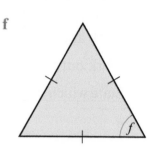

d
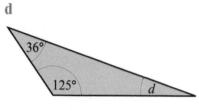

e
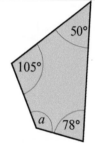

f
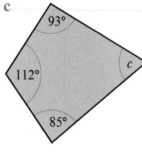

3 Look at each shape. Work out the size of each angle marked with a letter.

a
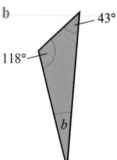

b

c

d
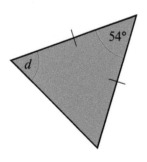

e
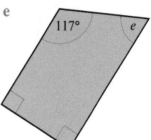

f
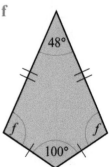

explanation 3

4 Look at each diagram. Calculate the size of each lettered angle.

Explain your methods clearly.

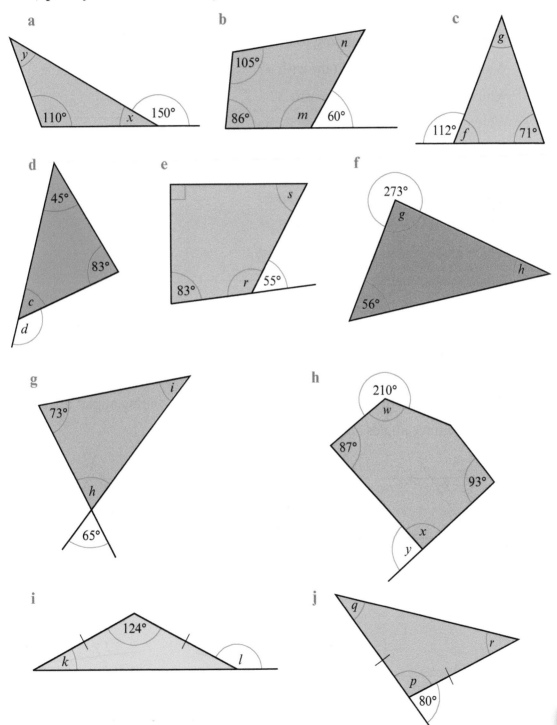

a

b

c

d

e

f

g

h

i

j

explanation 4a   explanation 4b

5 The diagram shows two parallel lines.
They are intersected by another straight line.

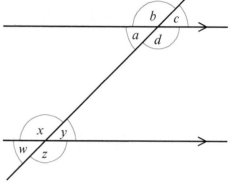

  a Which angle is alternate to *y*?

  b Which angle is corresponding to *a*?

  c Which angle is supplementary with *d*?

  d Which angle is vertically opposite *x*?

  e Which angle is on a straight line with *w*?

6 Look again at the diagram in question **5**.

  a Which angle rule links angles *d* and *x*?

  b Which angle rule links angles *c* and *y*?

  c Which angle rule links angles *a* and *x*?

  d Which angle rule links angles *b* and *d*?

  e Which angle rule links angles *c* and *d*?

7 For each diagram, calculate the size of the lettered angle.
State which angle rule you use. Choose from these.

  i alternate angles are equal   **ii** corresponding angles are equal

  iii supplementary angles add to 180°

a
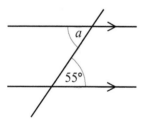

b
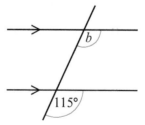

c
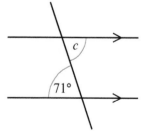

d
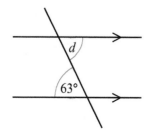

e
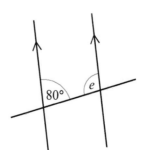

f
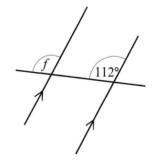

explanation 5

8 For each diagram, calculate the size of each lettered angle.

State which angle rule you use.

a

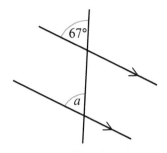

b

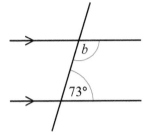

c

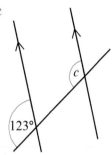

d

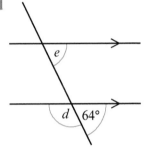

e

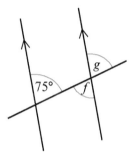

f

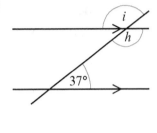

g

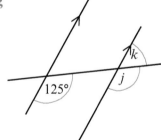

h

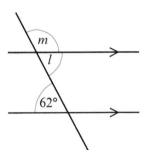

i

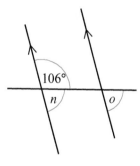

j

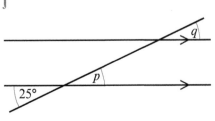

k

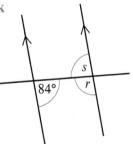

l

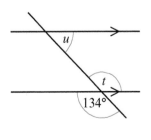

9 Calculate the size of each lettered angle.

Give reasons for your answers.

a

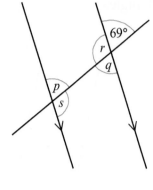

b

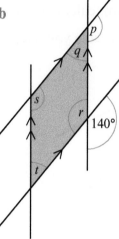

c

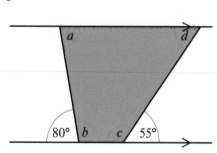

d

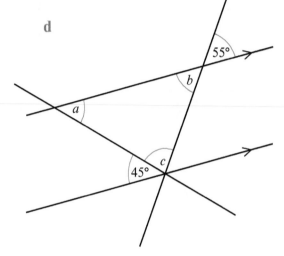

10 ABCD is a trapezium.

a How do you know that angle *d* is 35°?

b Find angle *e*.

c Find angle *f*.

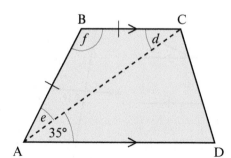

11   ABCD is a quadrilateral.

    a   Find angle x.

    b   Find angle y.

    c   Is the line DC parallel to AB? How do you know?

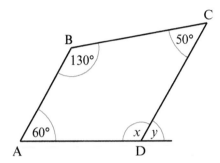

12   Six parallelograms are put together to make this shape.

    a   Find angle x.

    b   Find angle y.

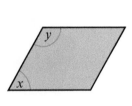
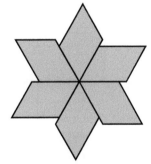

13   This shape is made from three yellow and three orange parallelograms.

    a   Find angle x.

    b   Find angle y.

    c   Find angle z.

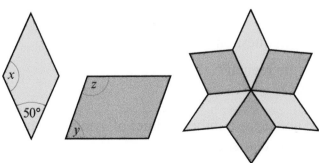

Polygons

- Identifying a regular shape and all of its symmetries
- Drawing an inscribed regular polygon
- Finding the exterior and interior angles of a regular polygon
- Finding the angle sum of a regular polygon
- Solving problems involving polygons

Keywords

You should know

explanation 1a   explanation 1b

1 Copy each shape. Draw any lines of symmetry.

a   b   c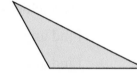

d   e    f

g    h 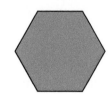   i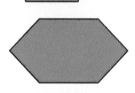

2 Look again at the shapes in question 1. Which of the shapes have rotation symmetry? State the orders of the rotation symmetry.

3 Look again at the shapes in question 1.

   a Which of the shapes are regular?

   b Name each shape.

   c What do you notice about the number of lines of symmetry and the order of rotation symmetry of regular shapes?

4 a   How many lines of symmetry does a regular octagon have?

b   What is the order of rotation symmetry for a regular octagon?

explanation 2a   explanation 2b   explanation 2c

5 The diagram shows an inscribed regular pentagon.

a   Explain how you work out that each angle, x, at the centre is 72°.

b   Why is triangle AOB isosceles?

c   Explain why angle y is 54°.

d   The sum of the angles in a pentagon is 540°. How can you use angle y to work this out?

e   Using a circle of radius 4 cm, draw an inscribed regular pentagon.

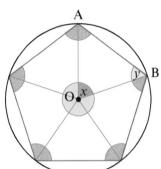

6 The diagram shows an inscribed regular hexagon.

a   Explain why each angle, x, at the centre is 60°.

b   What is the size of angle y?

c   What type of triangle is AOB?

d   Use angle y to work out the sum of the angles in a hexagon.

e   Using a circle of radius 4 cm, draw an inscribed regular hexagon.

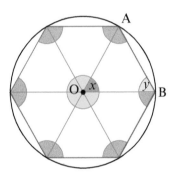

7 The diagram shows an inscribed regular octagon.

a   Find the size of angle x.

b   Using the fact that triangle AOB is isosceles, find angle y.

c   Use angle y to work out the sum of the angles in a octagon.

d   Using a circle of radius 4 cm, draw an inscribed regular octagon.

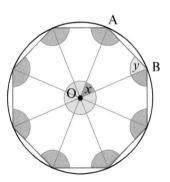

8 This question is about an inscribed regular decagon (10-sided polygon).

   a What is the size of each angle at the centre?

   b Using a circle of radius 4 cm, draw an inscribed regular decagon.

9 This question is about an inscribed regular dodecagon (12-sided polygon).

   a What is the size of each angle at the centre?

   b Using a circle of radius 4 cm, draw an inscribed regular dodecagon.

> explanation 3a   explanation 3b   explanation 3c

10 The diagram shows a regular pentagon.

   a What is the size of each exterior angle?

   b What is the size of each interior angle?

   c Work out its angle sum.

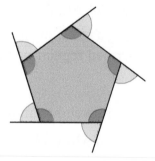

11 The diagram shows a regular octagon.

   a What is the size of each exterior angle?

   b What is the size of each interior angle?

   c Work out its angle sum.

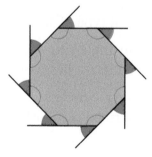

12 **a** How can you find the exterior angle of a regular polygon?

   b How can you use the exterior angle to work out an interior angle of a regular polygon?

   c How can you work out the angle sum of a regular polygon?

13 Copy and complete the table.

Regular polygon	Number of sides	Exterior angle	Interior angle	Angle sum
Equilateral triangle	3	120°	60°	180°
Square	4			
Pentagon	5			
Hexagon	6			
Octagon	8			
Decagon	10			
Dodecagon	12			
Icosagon	20			

*14 A regular polygon has interior angles of 170°.

a   What is the size of each exterior angle?

b   How many of the exterior angles make 360°?

c   How many sides does the polygon have?

d   How would you work out its angle sum?

*15 A regular polygon has interior angles of 160°.

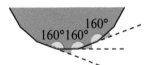

a   What is the size of each exterior angle?

b   How many of the exterior angles make 360°?

c   How many sides does the polygon have?

d   How would you work out its angle sum?

16 Use the fact that the angle sum of any pentagon is 540° to find angle *x*.

a

b

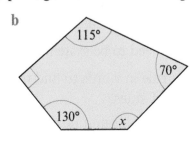

17 Use the fact that the angle sum of any hexagon is 720° to find angle *x*.

a

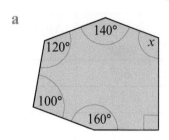

b

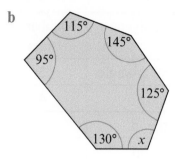

*18 The diagrams below show how you can find the angle sum of a pentagon by breaking it into triangles.

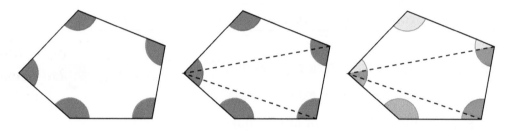

a Explain why the angle sum of a pentagon is 540°.
Use the diagrams and the fact that angles in a triangle add up to 180°.

b Use the same idea to show that the angle sum of a hexagon is 720°.

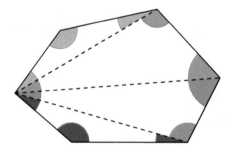

c What do you notice about the number of triangles a polygon breaks into compared to its number of sides?

You will need to be systematic. It might help you to draw a table.

d Write a rule in words to find the angle sum of a polygon if you know the number of sides.

Use your rule to find the angle sum of an irregular dodecagon (12 sides).

Collecting data

- Identifying what data to collect to answer a question
- Knowing how to collect data
- Organising data into grouped frequency tables

Keywords

You should know

explanation 1

1 To answer a question, you need to decide what data to collect and where it should come from.

Copy and complete the table. The first line has been done for you.

	Question	Data needed	Units and accuracy (where appropriate)	Where will data come from?
	How many hours of sport do pupils do in a week?	Number of hours of sport	Hours, to nearest half hour	Pupils at school
a	Which football team scored the most goals last season?			
b	Do tall people have longer legs than short people?			
c	Which supermarket has the cheapest prices?			
d	Do boys do more homework than girls?			
e	Which country has the largest population?			
f	How long do pupils take to travel to school?			
g	Is it warmer in Madrid or Rome?			

explanation 2a   explanation 2b

2 Liam wants to survey pupils at his school to find out what they think of school dinners. There are 1500 pupils in his school. He decides to ask everyone in the school.

Why isn't this a sensible idea?

3 Sasha wants to find out if boys or girls send the most text messages.

She puts this question on her questionnaire.

> How many text messages do you send?
> ☐ 0–10   ☐ 11–20   ☐ more than 20

a What is wrong with this question?

b Write an improved question.

4 Jelita wants to find out how much sport and what type of sport people play.

She wrote two questions.

> 1   How often do you play sport?   ☐ A lot   ☐ Not much
> 2   What sport do you play?   ☐ Football   ☐ Netball

a Explain what is wrong with each question.

b Write a better question each time.

5 Work with a partner.

a   **i** Write a question of your own to find out how much television your partner watches. Try out your question on your partner.

ii Was your partner able to answer your question easily?
If not, write an improved question and try that out.

Repeat steps **i** and **ii** to investigate these questions.

b How long your partner spends doing homework.

c What your partner thinks of school dinners.

d How far your partner travels to school.

6   Mel asks 24 of her friends to name their favourite crisp flavour.

She writes down their answers.

Ready Salted	Salt & Vinegar	Cheese & Onion	Cheese & Onion
Prawn Cocktail	Cheese & Onion	Beef	Salt & Vinegar
Ready Salted	Prawn Cocktail	Salt & Vinegar	Salt & Vinegar
Cheese & Onion	Cheese & Onion	Cheese & Onion	Ready Salted
Salt & Vinegar	Cheese & Onion	Ready Salted	Prawn Cocktail
Ready Salted	Ready Salted	Cheese & Onion	Beef

a   Copy and fill in this data collection sheet using Mel's data.

Crisp flavour	Tally	Frequency
Beef		
Cheese & Onion		
Prawn Cocktail		
Ready Salted		
Salt & Vinegar		

b   Which is the most popular flavour of crisp?

7   Design a data collection sheet for a survey to find out which subject pupils like best.

8   Design a data collection sheet for a survey to find out which supermarket most people use.

9   Design a data collection sheet for a survey to find out people's favourite pet.

10 Design a data collection sheet for a survey to find out how many times a month people go to the cinema.

11 a Design a data collection sheet for a survey of your choice.

b Use your data collection sheet to survey 15 people in your class.

c Are there any changes you think need to be made to your data collection sheet?

12 a Design a data collection sheet that can be used to record how many times each number occurs when a dice is rolled.

b Roll a dice 50 times and fill in your data collection sheet.

c Draw a bar chart of your results.

explanation 3

13 Anthony asked some of his friends how many emails they received that day. He put the results in a grouped frequency table.

Number of emails	Frequency
0–4	6
5–9	10
10–14	23
15–19	17
20–24	4

a How many friends did Anthony ask?

b How many friends received between 15 and 19 emails?

c How many friends received less than 10 emails?

14 These are the results for 26 students in a mathematics examination.

70	57	55	56	69	66	65	74	78	60	86	67	68
76	91	90	87	88	70	63	70	79	85	68	72	66

Copy and complete the grouped frequency table.

Mark	Tally	Frequency
50–59		
60–69		
70–79		
80–89		
90–99		

15 These are the heights to the nearest centimetre of 24 male students.

133	150	142	139	142	129	158	144	159	135	134	146
150	168	188	136	172	153	140	170	155	138	176	158

Copy and complete the grouped frequency table.

Height of student	Tally	Frequency
120–129		
130–139		

16 These are the times taken by 20 runners to run 100 m.
Times are measured in seconds correct to the nearest tenth of a second.

10.4	10.6	10.3	10.7	11.3	10.9	11.3	10.8	10.8	11.1
11.2	11.5	10.4	11.0	10.9	11.1	10.2	11.2	10.5	10.7

a Copy and complete the grouped frequency table.

Time (seconds)	Tally	Frequency
10.2–10.4		
10.5–10.7		

b Which class interval has the highest frequency?

47

Working with data

- Knowing which average to use for data
- Identifying the modal class interval for grouped data
- Calculating the mean from a frequency table

explanation 1

1 Jordan noted the number of texts he received each hour one Saturday afternoon.

3　　3　　4　　6　　9

Find these statistics for the number of texts he received.

　a　range　　　　　　　b　mode

　c　median　　　　　　d　mean

2 These are the numbers of red cards issued during six football matches.

3　　4　　0　　4　　6　　1

Find these statistics for the number of red cards issued.

　a　range

　b　mode

　c　median

　d　mean

3 Amy recorded how many siblings eight friends have.

4　　2　　2　　1　　1　　1　　0　　5

Find these statistics for the number of siblings.

　a　range　　　　　　　b　mode

　c　median　　　　　　d　mean

4 Hervey counted the number of emails he received each day for a week.

8   10   12   9   8   11   6

Find these statistics for the
number of emails.

a   range

b   mode

c   median

d   mean (correct to 1 decimal place)

5 These are the heights, in centimetres, of ten students in one class.

167   143   167   183   148   165   165   177   168   155

Find these statistics for the heights.

a   range

b   mode

c   median

d   mean

6 These are the marks of some pupils in an end-of-term test.

54   34   22   29   25   20   26   28   19   16   32   31   31   41   25

a   How many pupils took the test?

b   Work out the median mark.

c   Work out the mean mark. Give your answer correct to one decimal place.

(explanation 2)

7 Ten friends each write down their marks from a test.

9   9   8   3   6   8   3   2   3   4

a   Find the mode, median and mean of the test results.

b   Sahil says that the average mark is 5. Which average is Sahil using?

c   Gill says that the average mark is 5.5. Which average is Gill using?

d   John says that the average mark is 3. Which average is John using?

8 Which of the three averages, mean, median or mode, would be used in these cases?

   a Average age of pupils in Year 9

   b Average age in a family with six children under the age of 10, two parents aged 33 and 34 and one great-grandfather aged 98

   c Average shoe size in a class

   d Average number of children per family in the UK

   e Favourite flavour of ice cream in school

   f Average salary in a company where the manager has a salary of £5 000 000 per year

   g Average weight of a group of babies at birth

   h Most common colour of car in the staff car park

9 Six friends wrote down their shoe size.

   5   6   7   5   8   4

   Sarah says the average shoe size is $5\frac{1}{2}$.

   Emily says the average shoe size is 5.

   They are both correct. Explain why.

explanation 3a   explanation 3b   explanation 3c

10 The table shows the results of rolling a dice.

   a How many times was the dice rolled?

   b Find the mode.

   c Find the median.

Number on dice	Frequency
1	6
2	7
3	3
4	5
5	4
6	5

11 The table shows the number of pets owned by 15 families.

Number of pets	Frequency
0	6
1	2
2	1
3	0
4	5
5	1

a Find the mode.

b Find the median.

12 The table shows the number of lengths 13 pupils swam in 10 minutes.

Lengths swum in 10 minutes	Frequency
13	1
14	4
15	3
16	3
17	2

a Find the mode.

b Find the median.

13 The table shows the number of keys some adults had on their key rings.

Number of keys	Frequency
2	5
3	2
4	8
5	10

a How many key rings were there?

b Find the mode.

c Find the median.

14 The table shows the number of books some pupils had in their bags.

Books	Frequency
1	12
2	10
3	12
4	15
5	8
6	3

a How many pupils were surveyed?

b Find the mode.

c Find the median.

15 This table shows the weight of 19 athletes correct to the nearest kilogram.

Weight in kg	Frequency
60–64	1
65–69	7
70–74	4
75–79	6
80–84	1

Write the modal class.

16 The table shows the number of text messages received each day by Jo in February.

Number of texts	Frequency
0–4	2
5–9	7
10–14	4
15–19	7
20–24	8

Write the modal class.

17 The table shows the height, correct to the nearest centimetre, of forty 15-year-olds.

Height (cm)	Frequency
150–154	3
155–159	6
160–164	9
165–169	9
170–174	8
175–179	5

Write the modal class.

explanation 4

18 The table shows the number of goals scored by a football team in each of 20 matches.

Goals scored	Frequency	Goals scored × frequency
0	4	
1	3	
2	4	
3	6	
4	3	
Total		

a   Write the mode.

b   Copy and complete the table.

c   Work out the mean number of goals scored.

19 The table shows the results of spinning a spinner marked 1–4.

Score	Frequency	Score × frequency
1	5	
2	8	
3	4	
4	3	
Total		

a Copy and complete the table.

b How many times was the spinner spun?

c Work out the mean score.

20 The table shows the number of DVDs watched in the last month by 40 teachers.

a Write the mode.

b Work out the median.

c Work out the mean number of DVDs watched.

Number of DVDs	Frequency
0	3
1	6
2	10
3	6
4	15

21 The table shows the number of broken eggs in each of 40 boxes of eggs.

Number of broken eggs	Frequency
0	24
1	8
2	5
3	3

a Write the mode.

b Work out the median.

c Work out the mean number of broken eggs in a box.

Representing data

- Drawing a pie chart to represent data
- Determining whether two sets of data are correlated
- Drawing a line graph to see how data changes over time
- Representing data in a two-way table

Keywords

You should know

explanation 1a   explanation 1b   explanation 1c   explanation 1d

1 Jane drew some diagrams for her geography project.

Write the name of each type of diagram that Jane has drawn.

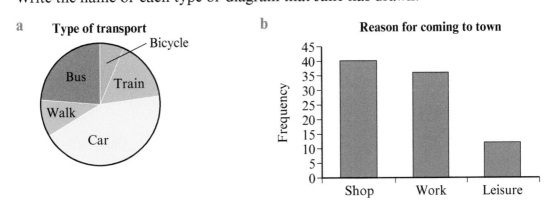

a   Type of transport

b   Reason for coming to town

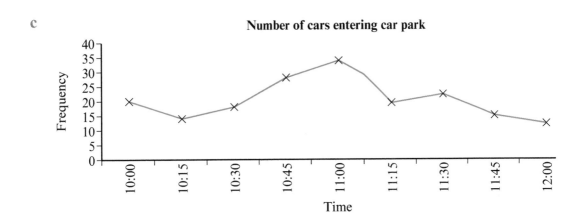

c   Number of cars entering car park

2 The table shows the favourite foods of 180 pupils.

a Work out the number of degrees in a pie chart that would represent 1 pupil.

b Copy and complete the table.

Favourite food	Frequency	Angle on pie chart
Chocolate	60	
Steak	35	
Pasta	45	
Crisps	40	
Total	180	

c Draw a pie chart to display the data.

3 The table shows the favourite type of music of 90 pupils.

a Work out the number of degrees that would represent 1 pupil.

b Copy and complete the table.

Favourite music	Frequency	Angle on pie chart
Rock	30	
Rap	15	
Jazz	10	
Reggae	15	
Blues	20	
Total	90	

c Draw a pie chart to display the data.

4 This table has been taken from a survey of school children.
It shows where sixty 11–14 year olds live.

a Work out the number of degrees in a pie chart that would represent 1 pupil.

b Copy and complete the table.

Where pupils live	Frequency	Angle on pie chart
Town	28	
Village	16	
City	12	
Other	4	
Total	60	

c Draw a pie chart to display the information.

5 This table shows the hair colour of 120 pupils.

Hair colour	Number of pupils	Angle on pie chart
Blond	30	
Brown	42	
Black	36	
Red	12	
Total		

a Work out the number of degrees in a pie chart that would represent 1 pupil.

b Copy and complete the table.

c Draw a pie chart to display the information.

6 This table shows the colour of 40 cars in a car park.

Draw a pie chart to display this information.

Colour of car	Number of cars
Blue	15
Red	7
Silver	9
White	3
Black	2
Other	4

7 This table shows the number of goals scored by a team in 20 football matches.

Draw a pie chart to display this information.

Number of goals	Frequency
0	6
1	5
2	2
3	5
4	2

explanation 2a   explanation 2b   explanation 2c

8 **a** Which of these scatter graphs shows positive correlation? Explain why.

   b Which of the graphs shows negative correlation? Explain why.

   c Which of the graphs shows no correlation? Explain why.

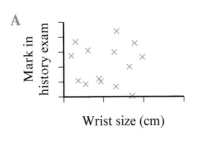

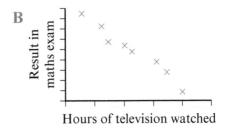

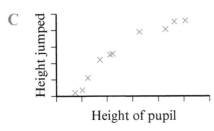

9 The table gives details about the age in years and the diameter of the trunk in inches of some grapefruit trees in an orchard.

Age of tree in years	8	7	10	6	7	8	5	9	10	5	6	6
Diameter of trunk in inches	6.5	5.7	7.1	5.5	6.2	6.2	4.2	6.6	7	4.6	5	5.2

   a Draw a graph with the horizontal axis going from 4 to 12 and the vertical axis going from 4 to 10. Scale your axes as shown.

   b Plot the points given in the table on your graph.

   c What type of correlation does your graph show?

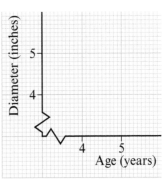

10 These are the results of 11 pupils in their maths examination.

Paper 1 non-calculator	21	16	16	30	38	23	32	25	28	40	31
Paper 2 calculator	18	14	19	28	34	14	31	22	30	35	31

a Draw a graph with the horizonal axis going from 0 to 50 and the vertical axis going from 0 to 40.
Scale your axes like this.

b Plot the points given in the table on your graph.

c Describe the correlation between the scores for paper 1 and paper 2.

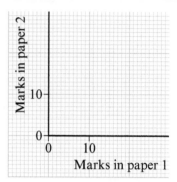

11 Here are the maths and art test scores for twelve pupils.

Maths	75	23	51	67	65	72	18	48	50	34	78	61
Art	27	72	43	31	36	22	65	45	61	75	29	30

a Draw a graph with both axes going from 0 to 80.
Scale your axes as shown.

b Plot the points given in the table on your graph.

c Describe the correlation between the marks for maths and art.

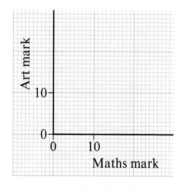

12 This scatter graph shows the class results in a mock examination and in the actual paper, five months later.

a Describe the correlation between the results in the two examinations.

b In which paper did most pupils do better? Explain your reasoning.

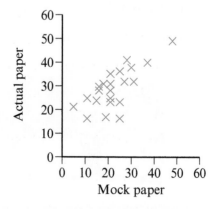

Mock and actual results

explanation 3

13 These are the monthly sales figures in thousands of pounds from a company.

Jan	Feb	Mar	Apr	May	Jun	Jul	Aug	Sep	Oct	Nov	Dec
54	62	56	59	67	61	58	55	54	50	52	66

a   Draw a line graph to display the data plotting the months on the
    horizontal axis and the sales figures on the vertical axis.

b   The company ran an advertising campaign from March to May.

   Do you think the advertising campaign was successful? Explain your answer.

14 The data shows the actual past population figures in millions for the UK and
   Italy and the forecasted populations up to the year 2050.

a   Plot the data as two line graphs on the same axes.
    Put year on the horizontal axis and population on the vertical axis.

Year	Population (millions) UK	Population (millions) Italy
1950	50	47
1960	52	50
1970	56	54
1980	56	56
1990	57	57
2000	60	58
2010	61	58
2020	63	57
2030	64	55
2040	64	53
2050	64	50

b   What is the predicted population in the UK and Italy in 2015?

c   Calculate the difference between the populations of the two countries for
    each year listed.

d   In which year will there be the greatest difference in the populations of
    the two countries?

15 These are the average monthly temperatures in degrees Celsius in London and Los Angeles.

   a Plot both sets of data as line graphs on the same axes.
Put the months on the horizontal axis and the temperature on the vertical axis.

	Jan	Feb	Mar	Apr	May	Jun	Jul	Aug	Sep	Oct	Nov	Dec
London (°C)	4	4	6	8	12	15	17	16	14	10	7	5
Los Angeles (°C)	20	21	21	23	24	27	29	30	28	26	23	20

   b What is the range of temperatures in London?

   c What is the range of temperatures in Los Angeles?

   d In which month is there the greatest difference between the temperature in London and the temperature in Los Angeles?

explanation 4a   explanation 4b

16 Chris conducted a survey in her year group.
She displayed her findings in this two-way table.

	Right-handed	Left-handed	Total
Girls	52	7	59
Boys	68	17	85
Total	120	24	144

   a How many pupils did she ask?

   b What question do you think she asked?

   c How many boys are there in the year group?

   d How many left-handed pupils are there in the year group?

   e How many of the girls are right-handed?

   f How many of the boys are left-handed?

17 Ian did a survey to find the favourite sandwich filling in his class.
He drew up this table to display his data.

	Ham	Tuna	Cheese	Salad	Total
Brown bread	6	2	3	2	13
White bread	7	4	4	1	16
Total	13	6	7	3	29

    a   How many people are there in Ian's class?

    b   How many people preferred white bread?

    c   How many people preferred salad sandwiches?

    d   How many people chose a cheese sandwich made with brown bread?

    e   How many more people prefer ham sandwiches than tuna sandwiches?

    f   What does the figure in yellow represent?

18 This table shows the type of book chosen by pupils from a school library.
Some of the table has been filled in.

    a   What does the figure highlighted in yellow represent?

    b   What does the figure highlighted in blue represent?

    c   Copy and complete the table.

	Fiction	Non-fiction	Total
Boys		45	96
Girls			
Total	88		146

19 This table shows the choice between
art and music of 52 pupils.
Some of the table has been filled in.

    a   What does the figure in pink
represent?

    b   What does the figure in lilac
represent?

    c   Copy and complete the table.

	Art	Music	Total
Boys	5		25
Girls	20	7	
Total			

20 The number of pupils absent from school one day is shown in this two-way table.

	Year 7	Year 8	Year 9	Year 10	Year 11	Total
Girls	8	6	5	6	3	28
Boys	7	8	8	5	5	33
Total	15	14	13	11	8	61

a How many Year 9 boys were absent?

b How many Year 10 girls were absent?

c How many Year 8 pupils were absent?

d How many boys were absent?

e How many more boys than girls were absent?

21 This table shows some data on when and where 100 people stayed for their summer holiday. Some of the table has been filled in.

	Hotel	Camping	Other	Total
July		11	5	20
August	15		8	
September		14		32
Total	28			100

a What does the figure in orange represent?

b What does the figure in blue represent?

c Copy and complete the table.

d How many people did not stay in a hotel?

e How many people went on holiday in either July or August?

Factors, multiples, primes and powers

- Writing a number as a product of prime factors
- Writing numbers using index notation
- Using index laws
- Finding common factors and the highest common factor (HCF)
- Finding common multiples and the lowest common multiple (LCM)

Keywords

You should know

explanation 1

1 Write all the factors of these numbers.

   a   18   b   30   c   56   d   75   e   64   f   100

2 Which of the numbers in the box is *not* a factor of the given number?

   a   72

8	36
3	16

   b   120

24	12	
	4	48

3 Write the first six multiples of each of these numbers.

   a   3   b   7   c   12   d   11   e   25

4 Which of the numbers in the box is *not* a multiple of the given number?

   a   4

16	20
25	
96	128

   b   7

28	35
49	
98	114

5 Find the first number greater than 25 that is a multiple of 6 *and* a factor of 96.

6 For each list write down the number that is *not* prime.

   a   1, 2, 3, 5, 7   b   7, 11, 13, 27

   c   2, 5, 11, 21, 23   d   7, 11, 17, 23, 25, 29

7 Explain why 2 is the only even number that is prime.

8 Are these numbers prime? Explain your answer.

a 43   b 57   c 61   d 85

---

explanation 2

9 Write the prime factors of each number.

a 30   b 45

c 66   d 110

> Remember to write only the factors that are prime numbers.

10 Copy and complete these factor trees.

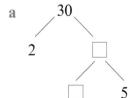

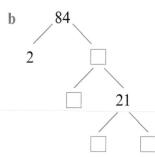

11 Use the factor trees in question **10** to write 30 and 84 as the product of primes.

a $30 = 2 \times \square \times 5$ b $84 = 2 \times \square \times \square \times \square$

12 Draw factor trees for these numbers.

a 45   b 80   c 100   d 252   e 368

13 Use the factor trees in question **12** to write each number as a product of prime factors.

---

explanation 3a   explanation 3b   explanation 3c

14 Write these using index notation.

a $2 \times 2 \times 2$ b $4 \times 4 \times 4 \times 4$ c $7 \times 7 \times 7 \times 7 \times 7 \times 7$

d $2 \times 2 \times 3 \times 3 \times 3$ e $3 \times 4 \times 4 \times 4 \times 4 \times 4$ f $6 \times 6 \times 7 \times 7 \times 8$

g $5 \times 6 \times 6 \times 6 \times 6 \times 7 \times 7 \times 8$ h $4 \times 4 \times 7 \times 7 \times 8 \times 9 \times 9 \times 10$

15 Write the products of prime factors that you found in question **13** using index notation.

16 Write each number as a product of primes using index notation.

a 72   b 96   c 150

17 Copy and complete this explanation of why $5^3 \times 5^4 = 5^7$.

$5^3 \times 5^4 = (\square \times \square \times \square) \times (\square \times \square \times \square \times \square) = \square$

18 Use the index laws to multiply these powers.

a $4^4 \times 4^5$ b $5^5 \times 5^6$ c $8^3 \times 8^6$ d $3^3 \times 3^0$

e $4^7 \times 4^8$ f $2^3 \times 2^2 \times 4^4$ g $3^5 \times 5^2 \times 3^2$ h $3^2 \times 4^3 \times 3^2$

19 Use the index laws to divide these powers.

a $4^8 \div 4^5$ b $7^7 \div 7^4$ c $3^8 \div 3^7$ d $9^5 \div 9^2$

e $5^5 \div 5^3$ f $3^3 \div 3^0$ g $4^8 \div 4^8$ h $3^{12} \div 3^2$

20 State whether each of these is true or false.
If it is false, explain what mistake has been made.

a $4^3 \times 4^2 = 4^6$ b $6^4 + 6^3 = 6^7$ c $5^2 \times 3^3 = 15^5$

d $3^5 \div 3^3 = 3^2$ e $2^4 - 2^2 = 2^2$ f $4^7 \div 4^0 = 4^7$

> explanation 4a   explanation 4b

21 a List all the factors of 48.

b List all the factors of 60.

c Write down the common factors of 48 and 60.

d What is the highest common factor (HCF) of 48 and 60?

22 a List the factors of 56 and 72.

b What is the HCF of 56 and 72?

23 Copy and complete the factor trees to find the HCF of 120 and 252.

a 120

2 □

2 □

□ 15

□ □

$120 = 2 \times 2 \times \square \times \square \times \square$

b 252

2 □

2 □

□ 21

□ □

$252 = 2 \times 2 \times \square \times \square \times \square$

c The HCF of 120 and 252 $= 2 \times 2 \times \square = \square$

24 Use factor trees, or any other method, to find the HCF of 84 and 100.

(explanation 5a) (explanation 5b)

25 a List the first six multiples of 5.

b List the first six multiples of 4.

c What is the lowest common multiple (LCM) of 5 and 4?

26 a List the first ten multiples of 8 and 9.

b What is the LCM of 8 and 9?

27 Copy and complete the factor trees to find the LCM of 20 and 50.

a 20

2 □

□ □

$20 = 2 \times \square \times \square$

b 50

2 □

□ □

$50 = 2 \times \square \times \square$

c The LCM of 20 and 50 $= 2 \times \square \times \square \times \square = \square$

28 Use factor trees, or any other method, to find the LCM of 84 and 100.

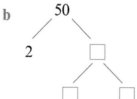
Use your working for question **24** to help.

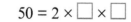

Adding and subtracting fractions

- Finding equivalent fractions
- Cancelling fractions to write them in their simplest form
- Converting decimals to fractions
- Converting fractions to decimals
- Adding and subtracting fractions with different denominators

Keywords

You should know

explanation 1a   explanation 1b

1 Use the diagram to help you find *one* equivalent fraction for each of these.

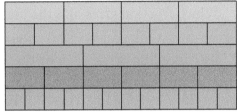

a $\dfrac{1}{3}$

b $\dfrac{1}{2}$

c $\dfrac{3}{12}$

d $\dfrac{4}{6}$

e $\dfrac{9}{12}$

f $\dfrac{4}{8}$

2 Copy and complete these equivalent fractions.

a $\dfrac{1}{2} = \dfrac{\square}{4} = \dfrac{3}{\square} = \dfrac{\square}{8} = \dfrac{5}{\square} = \dfrac{\square}{12}$

b $\dfrac{1}{3} = \dfrac{2}{\square} = \dfrac{\square}{9} = \dfrac{4}{\square} = \dfrac{5}{\square}$

c $\dfrac{4}{5} = \dfrac{\square}{10} = \dfrac{16}{\square} = \dfrac{20}{\square} = \dfrac{\square}{100}$

d $\dfrac{3}{4} = \dfrac{6}{\square} = \dfrac{\square}{16} = \dfrac{18}{\square} = \dfrac{\square}{40}$

3 Work out what number goes in each box to make an equivalent fraction.

Write the pairs of fractions.

a $\overset{\times 4}{\frown}$ $\dfrac{1}{5} = \dfrac{\square}{20}$ $\underset{\times 4}{\smile}$

b $\overset{\times 5}{\frown}$ $\dfrac{5}{6} = \dfrac{25}{\square}$ $\underset{\times 5}{\smile}$

c $\overset{\div 3}{\frown}$ $\dfrac{12}{21} = \dfrac{\square}{7}$ $\underset{\div 3}{\smile}$

d $\overset{\times \square}{\frown}$ $\dfrac{\square}{11} = \dfrac{18}{33}$ $\underset{\times \square}{\smile}$

e $\overset{\times \square}{\frown}$ $\dfrac{4}{10} = \dfrac{40}{\square}$ $\underset{\times \square}{\smile}$

f $\overset{\div 8}{\frown}$ $\dfrac{24}{32} = \dfrac{\square}{4}$ $\underset{\div 8}{\smile}$

g $\overset{\div \square}{\frown}$ $\dfrac{45}{63} = \dfrac{5}{\square}$ $\underset{\div \square}{\smile}$

h $\overset{\times \square}{\frown}$ $\dfrac{\square}{15} = \dfrac{35}{75}$ $\underset{\times \square}{\smile}$

4 In Sara's class 5 out of 9 girls play a musical instument.

In Zoe's class 14 out 27 girls play a musical instrument.

Write these proportions as fractions.

Use equivalent fractions with the same denominator to work out which class has the greater fraction of girls that play a musical instrument.

5 Dev's friend Karla said that she would give him either $\frac{7}{12}$ or $\frac{5}{8}$ of a large bar of chocolate.

Dev wanted to get the bigger piece.

Use equivalent fraction with the same denominators to compare these fractions.

Which fraction gives him the bigger piece?

6 By cancelling, write each of these fractions in its lowest terms.

a $\frac{15}{25}$ b $\frac{16}{18}$ c $\frac{25}{100}$ d $\frac{35}{77}$ e $\frac{50}{75}$

f $\frac{24}{56}$ g $\frac{48}{96}$ h $\frac{60}{66}$ i $\frac{45}{105}$ j $\frac{44}{132}$

7 Find the odd one out in each set of fractions.

a $\frac{3}{4}, \frac{30}{40}, \frac{24}{30}, \frac{12}{16}, \frac{75}{100}$

b $\frac{3}{5}, \frac{13}{20}, \frac{15}{25}, \frac{36}{60}, \frac{21}{35}$

c $\frac{1}{7}, \frac{10}{70}, \frac{9}{64}, \frac{4}{28}, \frac{12}{84}$

d $\frac{2}{9}, \frac{22}{99}, \frac{18}{81}, \frac{15}{90}, \frac{6}{27}$

8 Shona got these marks for her end-of-topic tests.

Maths $\frac{16}{20}$ English $\frac{24}{30}$ History $\frac{20}{25}$ Chemistry $\frac{35}{50}$ Biology $\frac{32}{40}$

Which of her test results is the odd one out?

(explanation 2a)   (explanation 2b)

9 Write each decimal as a fraction in its simplest form.

a 0.9   b 0.6   c 0.25   d 0.12   e 0.65   f 0.88

g 0.08   h 0.002   i 0.375   j 0.023   k 0.095   l 0.001

10 Write these fractions as decimals.

a $\dfrac{3}{10}$ b $\dfrac{12}{100}$ c $\dfrac{205}{1000}$ d $\dfrac{12}{25}$ e $\dfrac{3}{4}$

f $\dfrac{17}{20}$ g $\dfrac{18}{50}$ h $\dfrac{52}{250}$ i $\dfrac{123}{500}$ j $\dfrac{20}{125}$

Use a calculator for the divisions in questions **11** to **13**.

11 Write these fractions as decimals using division.

a $\dfrac{3}{8}$ b $\dfrac{7}{8}$ c $\dfrac{19}{40}$ d $\dfrac{48}{75}$ e $\dfrac{14}{16}$

12 Write these fractions as decimals using division.

Write recurring decimals to 2 d.p.

a $\dfrac{2}{3}$ b $\dfrac{5}{12}$ c $\dfrac{3}{11}$ d $\dfrac{4}{9}$ e $\dfrac{17}{30}$

13 Liam did a survey of how pupils travelled to school.
He recorded the results in a table.

Method of travel	Walk	Bus	Train	Car
Number of pupils	19	37	13	21

a How many pupils did he survey?

b What fraction of pupils travelled to school using each method?

c Change each fraction you found in part b into a decimal rounded to 2 d.p.

explanation 3a   explanation 3b

14 Change these mixed numbers to improper fractions.

a $1\dfrac{2}{3}$ b $3\dfrac{1}{2}$ c $2\dfrac{2}{5}$ d $5\dfrac{9}{10}$ e $4\dfrac{3}{11}$

f $3\dfrac{16}{25}$ g $7\dfrac{9}{20}$ h $2\dfrac{19}{50}$ i $1\dfrac{11}{15}$ j $2\dfrac{9}{13}$

15 Change these improper fractions into mixed numbers.

Write each fraction in its lowest terms.

a $\dfrac{8}{5}$ b $\dfrac{19}{3}$ c $\dfrac{32}{7}$ d $\dfrac{15}{2}$ e $\dfrac{73}{20}$

f $\dfrac{27}{6}$ g $\dfrac{45}{12}$ h $\dfrac{50}{15}$ i $\dfrac{58}{8}$ j $\dfrac{185}{25}$

16 Match each improper fraction in box A with the correct mixed number in box B.

Box A

$\dfrac{37}{7}$ $\qquad$ $\dfrac{71}{7}$ $\qquad$ $\dfrac{48}{7}$

$\dfrac{163}{30}$ $\qquad$ $\dfrac{137}{30}$ $\qquad$ $\dfrac{159}{30}$

Box B

$4\dfrac{17}{30}$ $\qquad$ $6\dfrac{6}{7}$ $\qquad$ $5\dfrac{13}{30}$

$5\dfrac{2}{7}$ $\qquad$ $5\dfrac{9}{30}$ $\qquad$ $10\dfrac{1}{7}$

explanation 4a   **explanation 4b**

17 Add each set of fractions.

Write the answer in its simplest form.

a $\dfrac{3}{7}+\dfrac{2}{7}$ b $\dfrac{3}{10}+\dfrac{5}{10}$ c $\dfrac{8}{25}+\dfrac{13}{25}$ d $\dfrac{11}{20}+\dfrac{7}{20}$

e $\dfrac{1}{12}+\dfrac{3}{12}+\dfrac{5}{12}$ f $\dfrac{2}{9}+\dfrac{4}{9}+\dfrac{5}{9}$ g $\dfrac{15}{22}+\dfrac{13}{22}+\dfrac{21}{22}$ h $\dfrac{3}{32}+\dfrac{18}{32}+\dfrac{23}{32}$

18 Work out these subtractions.

Write the answers in their lowest terms.

a $\dfrac{12}{15}-\dfrac{8}{15}$ b $\dfrac{7}{8}-\dfrac{5}{8}$ c $\dfrac{23}{25}-\dfrac{3}{25}$ d $\dfrac{27}{40}-\dfrac{13}{40}$

19 Add each pair of fractions. First find equivalent fractions so both fractions have the same denominator. Write the answer in its simplest form.

a $\dfrac{1}{3}+\dfrac{1}{6}$ b $\dfrac{2}{5}+\dfrac{3}{10}$ c $\dfrac{7}{12}+\dfrac{4}{24}$ d $\dfrac{8}{15}+\dfrac{2}{5}$

e $\dfrac{2}{5}+\dfrac{2}{3}$ f $\dfrac{7}{10}+\dfrac{3}{4}$ g $\dfrac{7}{8}+\dfrac{3}{5}$ h $\dfrac{7}{12}+\dfrac{1}{5}$

i $\dfrac{4}{15}+\dfrac{1}{2}$ j $\dfrac{4}{9}+\dfrac{7}{11}$ k $\dfrac{9}{10}+\dfrac{5}{8}$ l $\dfrac{2}{6}+\dfrac{3}{7}$

20 On one day last week $\frac{1}{8}$ of the pupils in a class were away sick and $\frac{2}{5}$ were on a history trip. What fraction of the class was absent from school?

21 Between them, Paul, Sam and Daisy sold all the raffle tickets for a charity fund.

Paul sold $\frac{1}{4}$ of the tickets and Sam sold $\frac{3}{7}$ of the tickets.

What fraction of tickets did Daisy sell?

22 Work out these subtractions. First find equivalent fractions so both fractions have the same denominator. Write the answer in its simplest form.

a $\frac{5}{6} - \frac{1}{2}$ b $\frac{11}{12} - \frac{1}{3}$ c $\frac{13}{15} - \frac{3}{5}$ d $\frac{5}{9} - \frac{4}{18}$

e $\frac{4}{5} - \frac{1}{4}$ f $\frac{6}{7} - \frac{2}{3}$ g $\frac{8}{11} - \frac{1}{4}$ h $\frac{7}{8} - \frac{2}{5}$

i $\frac{7}{9} - \frac{3}{8}$ j $\frac{11}{15} - \frac{2}{4}$ k $\frac{7}{12} - \frac{2}{5}$ l $\frac{19}{25} - \frac{2}{3}$

23 Mica has a $\frac{1}{2}$ litre of milk in a jug.

She pours $\frac{2}{5}$ litre of milk from the jug into a glass.

How much milk is left in the jug?

24 Chef Danny has $\frac{3}{4}$ kg of apples.

He makes an apple pie and uses $\frac{3}{5}$ kg of apples.

How many kilograms of apples will he have left?

25 Mr Davis left all his money to his three children.

His eldest was left $\frac{4}{9}$ of the total and the youngest got $\frac{1}{4}$.

What fraction did the other child get?

26 Teri put down a $\frac{1}{5}$ deposit on her new TV and paid off an additional $\frac{5}{12}$ in the first year.

What fraction of the total has she still got to pay?

Multiplying and dividing fractions

- Finding fractions of whole numbers
- Multiplying and dividing whole numbers by fractions
- Multiplying a fraction by a fraction
- Dividing a fraction by a fraction

Keywords

You should know

explanation 1a · explanation 1b

1 Find these amounts.

a $\frac{3}{10}$ of 40

b $\frac{4}{5}$ of 35

c $\frac{5}{7}$ of 42

d $\frac{3}{8}$ of 64

e $\frac{7}{11}$ of 110

f $\frac{3}{5}$ of 75

g $\frac{11}{15}$ of 45

h $\frac{9}{20}$ of 80

i $\frac{7}{12}$ of 84

j $\frac{11}{25}$ of 150

k $\frac{14}{60}$ of 120

l $\frac{19}{40}$ of 280

m $\frac{35}{36}$ of 144

n $\frac{23}{27}$ of 108

o $\frac{39}{44}$ of 220

p $\frac{36}{55}$ of 210

2 Suriya earned £360 last week. She saves $\frac{2}{9}$ of her salary every week.

How much did she save last week?

3 A day on Jupiter is about $\frac{3}{8}$ of a day on Earth.

How many hours are there in a Jupiter day?

4 This recipe for Lemon Pepper Chicken serves 8 people.

Lemon Pepper Chicken	
1 kg chicken	400 g chopped onion
560 g green pepper	4 lemons
48 g butter	80 g flour
1.2 litres chicken stock	2 handfuls of fresh herbs, chopped

Remember
1 kg = 1000 g
1 litre = 1000 ml

How much of each ingredient will you need for 5 people?

5 Work out these multiplications.

a $\frac{1}{8} \times 32$ b $\frac{1}{12} \times 60$ c $45 \times \frac{2}{5}$ d $\frac{5}{9} \times 54$

e $48 \times \frac{3}{8}$ f $\frac{3}{8} \times 24$ g $\frac{5}{14} \times 42$ h $\frac{26}{50} \times 150$

i $\frac{11}{15} \times 45$ j $\frac{15}{20} \times 60$ k $\frac{12}{25} \times 100$ l $\frac{14}{30} \times 120$

6 One small jug holds $\frac{2}{5}$ litre of juice.

How much juice will be needed to fill 15 jugs?

explanation 2a explanation 2b

7 Work these out. Cancel first if possible.

a $\frac{2}{5} \times \frac{2}{7}$ b $\frac{2}{3} \times \frac{4}{5}$ c $\frac{3}{4} \times \frac{6}{7}$ d $\frac{4}{9} \times \frac{5}{12}$

e $\frac{10}{11} \times \frac{7}{20}$ f $\frac{7}{16} \times \frac{8}{9}$ g $\frac{7}{9} \times \frac{27}{30}$ h $\frac{21}{25} \times \frac{3}{7}$

8 Find three different pairs of fractions that multiply to give $\frac{15}{36}$.

9 Ben spent $\frac{1}{2}$ of his pocket money last week.

He used $\frac{1}{2}$ of the money to buy a new DVD.

What fraction of his pocket money did he spend on the DVD?

10 In a test Claire answered $\frac{5}{6}$ of the questions.

She got $\frac{4}{5}$ of her answers correct.

a What fraction of questions did she get correct?

b There were 60 questions in the test.
How many did she answer correctly?

explanation 3a   explanation 3b

11 Rewrite these divisions as multiplications and then solve them.

a $13 \div \frac{1}{6}$

b $24 \div \frac{1}{5}$

c $17 \div \frac{1}{10}$

d $24 \div \frac{3}{4}$

e $25 \div \frac{5}{6}$

f $42 \div \frac{7}{10}$

g $36 \div \frac{9}{11}$

h $63 \div \frac{7}{8}$

i $75 \div \frac{25}{30}$

j $114 \div \frac{6}{10}$

12 A rope is 18 m long. It is divided into pieces that are $\frac{2}{5}$ m long.

How many pieces of rope will there be?

13 A ferry completes a crossing every $\frac{2}{3}$ of an hour.

What is the greatest number of crossings it could make in 24 hours?

explanation 4

14 Invert each of these fractions.

a $\frac{2}{3}$

b $\frac{6}{7}$

c $\frac{12}{25}$

d $\frac{34}{50}$

e $\frac{19}{100}$

f $\frac{203}{520}$

15 Rewrite these divisions as multiplications and then solve them.

a $\frac{4}{7} \div \frac{2}{3}$

b $\frac{5}{6} \div \frac{3}{4}$

c $\frac{9}{10} \div \frac{3}{7}$

d $\frac{2}{9} \div \frac{4}{5}$

e $\frac{11}{12} \div \frac{3}{5}$

f $\frac{8}{11} \div \frac{5}{9}$

g $\frac{12}{15} \div \frac{5}{8}$

h $\frac{11}{20} \div \frac{3}{8}$

16 Indira had $\frac{17}{20}$ kg of apples.

She divided the apples into bags containing $\frac{3}{10}$ kg each.

How many bags of apples did she get?

17 Find three different pairs of fractions which give the answer $\frac{4}{9}$ when one is divided by the other.

Solving equations (1)

- Using a function machine to represent an expression
- Solving equations involving one operation
- Solving equations involving two operations
- Solving equations involving brackets

Keywords

You should know

---

explanation 1

1 Write the missing functions to map the input x to the given outputs.

a $x \rightarrow \boxed{} \rightarrow x + 6$

b $x \rightarrow \boxed{} \rightarrow x - 4$

c $x \rightarrow \boxed{} \rightarrow 5x$

d $x \rightarrow \boxed{} \rightarrow \dfrac{x}{2}$

2 Write the inverse of each operation.

a Add 6   b Multiply by 5   c Subtract 1   d Divide by 2

e $+ 5$ f $\times 6$ g $\div 3$ h $- 9$

3 Look at each function machine.
What is the missing operation that will make the output map back to the input?

a $x \rightarrow \boxed{+ 2} \rightarrow x + 2$

    $x \leftarrow \boxed{} \leftarrow x + 2$

b $x \rightarrow \boxed{- 6} \rightarrow x - 6$

    $x \leftarrow \boxed{} \leftarrow x - 6$

c $x \rightarrow \boxed{\times 3} \rightarrow 3x$

    $x \leftarrow \boxed{} \leftarrow 3x$

d $x \rightarrow \boxed{\div 4} \rightarrow \dfrac{x}{4}$

    $x \leftarrow \boxed{} \leftarrow \dfrac{x}{4}$

4 Use inverse operations to make each of these correct.

a $x + 1$

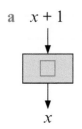

x

b $x - 4$

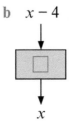

x

c $3x$

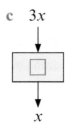

x

d $x - 6$

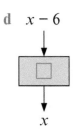

x

e $\dfrac{x}{2}$

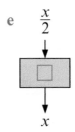

x

f $7x$

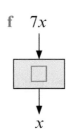

x

5 Copy and complete these.

a $x - 2 \ = \ 6$

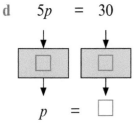

$x \ = \ \square$

b $\dfrac{x}{3} \ = \ 12$

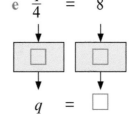

$x \ = \ \square$

c $g + 7 \ = \ 12$

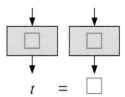

$g \ = \ \square$

d $5p \ = \ 30$

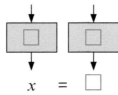

$p \ = \ \square$

e $\dfrac{q}{4} \ = \ 8$

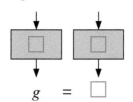

$q \ = \ \square$

f $t - 6 \ = \ 11$

$t \ = \ \square$

6 Solve these equations.

a $2x = 16$

b $n + 10 = 22$

c $y - 4 = 12$

d $q + 14 = 29$

e $t - 5 = 20$

f $4m = 32$

g $\frac{a}{2} = 12$

h $8 + k = 17$

i $\frac{r}{10} = 2$

j $2p = 15$

k $\frac{1}{2}h = 6$

l $w + 5 = 12$

| explanation 3a | explanation 3b |

7 Write the missing functions to map each input to the given output.

a $x \rightarrow$  $2x + 1$ b $r \rightarrow \square \rightarrow \square \rightarrow 3r - 7$

c $p \rightarrow$  $\frac{p}{4} - 2$ d $m \rightarrow \square \rightarrow \square \rightarrow 4m - 5$

e $t \rightarrow \square \rightarrow \square \rightarrow \frac{t}{2} + 6$ f $s \rightarrow \square \rightarrow \square \rightarrow 5s - 1$

8 Make these function machines and reverse function machines correct.
Write the missing operations.

a $x \rightarrow \square \rightarrow \square \rightarrow 3x + 2$ b $r \rightarrow \square \rightarrow \square \rightarrow 4r - 5$

$x \leftarrow \square \leftarrow \square \leftarrow 3x + 2$ $r \leftarrow \square \leftarrow \square \leftarrow 4r - 5$

c $m \rightarrow \square \rightarrow \square \rightarrow 5m - 3$ d $p \rightarrow \square \rightarrow \square \rightarrow \frac{p}{3} + 6$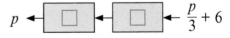

$m \leftarrow \square \leftarrow \square \leftarrow 5m - 3$ $p \leftarrow \square \leftarrow \square \leftarrow \frac{p}{3} + 6$

9 Copy and complete these.
Use inverse operations to map each expression to x.

a $2x + 3$

-3

$\downarrow$

$2x$

$\downarrow$

x

b $3x + 2$

$\downarrow$

$3x$

$\downarrow$

x

c $\dfrac{x}{2} - 1$

$\dfrac{x}{2}$

$\downarrow$

x

d $5x - 3$

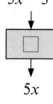

$5x$

$\downarrow$

x

e $4x - 5$

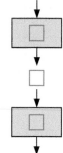

x

f $\dfrac{x}{3} + 6$

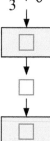

x

g $7x - 8$

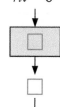

x

h $\dfrac{x}{4} + 1$

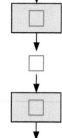

x

| explanation 4 |

10 Copy and complete these.

a $2x + 8 = 24$

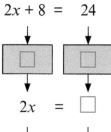

$2x = \square$

$x = \square$

b $4x - 11 = 9$

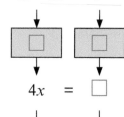

$4x = \square$

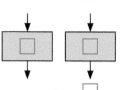

$x = \square$

c $\dfrac{x}{2} - 3 = 6$

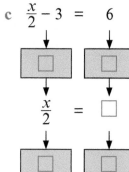

$\dfrac{x}{2} = \square$

$x = \square$

80

11 Copy and complete these.

a $4x - 3 = 21$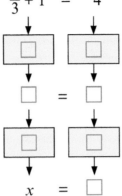

b $\frac{x}{3} + 1 = 4$

c $\frac{x}{4} + 5 = 8$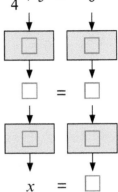

12 Check your answers to questions **10** and **11** using substitution.

13 Solve these equations. Check your answers, using substitution.

a $3x - 10 = 5$

b $2x + 12 = 20$

c $\frac{x}{2} - 6 = 4$

d $2g + 5 = 19$

e $\frac{p}{2} - 10 = 2$

f $\frac{x}{5} + 2 = 12$

g $4t - 5 = 23$

h $6h + 7 = 25$

i $\frac{q}{2} - 4 = 8$

j $2y + 12 = 28$

k $3n - 14 = 22$

l $\frac{t}{2} + 9 = 21$

m $5g - 3 = 32$

n $\frac{d}{3} + 6 = 8$

o $4x + 12 = 14$

> **explanation 5**

14 Expand the brackets in these expressions.

a $2(x + 6)$

b $3(n - 8)$

c $6(t + 2)$

d $10(h + 3)$

e $6(p - 1)$

f $7(b - 3)$

g $3(2x - 4)$

h $5(3n + 7)$

i $2(4t + 5)$

15 Copy and complete these. Check your answers by substitution.

a $2(x + 5) =$ 34

$2x + 10 =$ 34

$\square = \square$

$x = \square$

b $3(x + 2) =$ 12

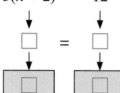

$\square = \square$

$x = \square$

c $2(x - 5) =$ 30

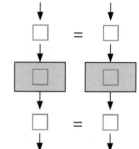

$\square = \square$

$x = \square$

d $3(x - 4) =$ 12

$\square = \square$

$\square = \square$

$x = \square$

e $4(x + 1) =$ 12

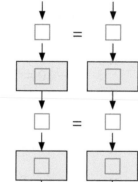

$\square = \square$

$x = \square$

f $6(x - 5) =$ 18

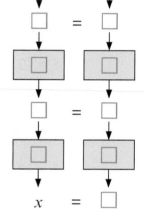

$\square = \square$

$x = \square$

16 Solve these equations.

a $3(x + 2) = 12$

b $4(t - 3) = 28$

c $5(m + 3) = 25$

d $2(n - 4) = 16$

e $3(p + 1) = 15$

f $5(y - 2) = 35$

g $4(2p + 3) = 44$

h $2(3q - 4) = 16$

i $5(2w - 4) = 60$

17 Solve these equations.

a $4x + 6 = 30$

b $3(x - 2) = 30$

c $5x - 4 = 34$

d $x - 8 = 30$

e $2(x + 6) = 28$

f $2x + 6 = 28$

g $3(4x - 2) = 66$

h $\frac{x}{2} - 8 = 15$

i $\frac{x}{3} + 2 = 8$

Formulae

- Substituting values into a formula
- Writing a formula using words
- Writing a formula using algebra

explanation 1

1 Daniel delivers the local paper on a Saturday.
   His pay depends on how many papers he delivers. He uses this formula:

   Total pay = pay per paper × number of papers delivered

   Daniel delivers 150 papers on a Saturday.

   He is paid 10p for delivering each paper.

   Use Daniel's formula to work out his total pay for working on Saturday.

2 Gabrielle buys some books online. She uses this formula:

   Total cost = cost of one book × number of books bought + cost of postage

   Gabrielle buys 3 books at £3.99 each.

   The total cost of postage is £3.00.

   Use Gabrielle's formula to work out how much money she spends.

3 Four friends are planning a trip to a bowling alley.
   They want to know how much it will cost. They use this formula:

   Total cost = cost of a game × number of games
                + cost of shoe hire × number of people

   The cost of a game is £3.00. They want to play four games.

   The cost of shoe hire is £0.50 per person.

   a Use the formula to work out the total cost of the four friends' trip to the
      bowling alley.

   b Write a word formula to work out the cost per person from the total cost.

   c Use your formula to work out how much each person pays.

4 Mrs Green runs the school shop. She buys a box of 200 pencils for £12.00.
She sells the pencils for 20p each. She uses this formula:

> Total profit = number of pencils sold × cost of one pencil − cost of the box

a Mrs Green sold 150 pencils in September.
Use her formula to work out the profit she made in September.

b How much profit will she make when she has sold all of the pencils from the box?

5 Mr Smith is organising a theatre trip for some students.
He works out how much to charge each person. He uses this formula:

> Cost per person = cost of one ticket + cost of hiring coach ÷ number of people

The cost of a theatre ticket is £12.00 per person.

The cost of hiring the coach is £150.

a There are 30 people going on the trip altogether.

Use Mr Smith's formula to work out the cost per person.

b If there were 50 people going on the trip, two coaches would have to be hired.
Work out the cost per person if 50 people went on the trip.

explanation 2

6 The cost of a car service is given by the formula $C = P + 40n$.

C is the cost in pounds of the service.

P is the cost in pounds of the replacement parts.

n is the number of hours that the job takes to complete.

a Calculate C when $P = 75$ and $n = 3$.

b Calculate C when $P = 150$ and $n = 5$.

7 The cost of buying a new car is given by the formula $C = D + 500n$.

C is the cost in pounds of the car.

D is the cost in pounds of the deposit.

n is the number of monthly instalments.

a Calculate C when $D = 4000$ and $n = 24$.

b Calculate C when $D = 6000$ and $n = 18$.

8 Jason has a set of football stickers and decides to give them to his younger brothers.

Jason has S stickers and 3 younger brothers. Each brother receives B stickers.

a Write a word formula for the number of stickers that each brother receives.

b Write a formula using the letters S and B.

c If $S = 36$, find the value of B.

9 Anna and Charlotte share a bag of sweets.

There are S sweets in the bag.

Anna takes A sweets.

Charlotte has the number of sweets left, C.

a Write a word formula for the number of sweets that Charlotte has.

b Write a formula using the letters C, S and A.

c If $S = 30$ and $A = 12$, find the value of C.

10 Jake and his friends want to go to the football match.

It costs £M for each match ticket and £3 for each bus fare.

There are C children altogether.

The total cost is £T.

a Write a word formula for the total cost
   for the friends to go to the football match.

b Write a formula using the letters T, M and C.

c If $M = 10$ and $C = 4$, find the value of T.

11 Philippa took part in a 10-mile fun run to raise money for charity.

Some people sponsored Philippa for taking part and other people sponsored her per mile.

Altogether she was sponsored £S for taking part and £P per mile.
The total amount of money she raised was £T.

a Write a word formula for the total amount of money she raised.

b Write your formula using the letters T, S and P.

c If $S = £50$ and $P = £30$, find the value of T.

explanation 3

12 Use the formula $F = ma$ to find F when $m = 2$ and $a = 8$.

13 Use the formula $s = \dfrac{d}{t}$ to find s when $d = 18$ and $t = 6$.

14 Use the formula $v = u + at$ to find v when $u = 4$, $a = 2$ and $t = 10$.

15 Use the formula $p = q + \dfrac{a}{t}$ to find p when $q = 5$, $a = 8$ and $t = 2$.

16 Use the formula $d = \dfrac{e + f}{g}$ to find d when $e = 8$, $f = 10$ and $g = 3$.

17 Albert Einstein worked out the famous formula $E = mc^2$.

When $m = 2$ and $c = 5$, explain why $E = 50$.

explanation 4a   explanation 4b

18 The diagram shows a triangle.

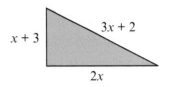

a Explain why the formula for the perimeter P of this triangle is $P = 6x + 5$.

b Use the formula $P = 6x + 5$ to find the perimeter when $x = 10$ cm.

19 A rectangle has length l and width w.

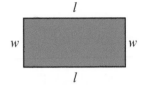

a Explain why the formula for the perimeter P of this rectangle is $P = 2(l + w)$.

b Use your formula to find the perimeter when $l = 12$ cm and $w = 7$ cm.

c Explain why the formula for the area A of this rectangle is $A = lw$.

d Use your formula to find the area when $l = 12$ cm and $w = 7$ cm.

20 The diagram shows a parallelogram.

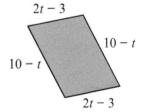

a Explain why the formula for the perimeter P of this parallelogram is $P = 2(t + 7)$.

b Use your formula to find the perimeter when $t = 8$ cm.

21 The diagram shows angles x and y making one full turn.

a Write a formula to find y.

b Use your formula to find y when $x = 135°$.

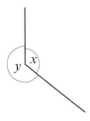

22 The diagram shows angles x and y in an isosceles triangle.

a Write a formula to find y.

b Use your formula to find y when $x = 65°$.

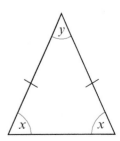

Translations, reflections and rotations

- Identifying congruent shapes
- Translating a shape on a coordinate grid
- Reflecting in vertical, horizontal and diagonal lines
- Rotating a shape about a centre of rotation
- Describing reflections, rotations and translations

Keywords

You should know

explanation 1a   explanation 1b

1   The diagram is on square dotted paper.
    It shows a square 5 units long and 5 units wide.
    The square has been split into two congruent shapes.

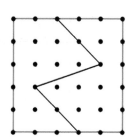

   a   Draw a square like this on square dotted paper.
       Split the square to make two more congruent shapes.

   b   By drawing more squares like this, find three more
       different ways to split the square into two congruent
       shapes.

2   Look at the shapes in the grid. Which shapes are congruent to shape X?

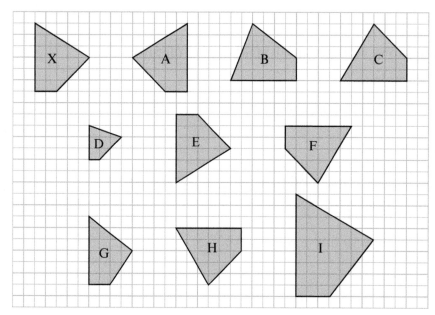

3 The diagram shows a tessellation made from a quadrilateral.

  a Copy and complete the tessellation.
  Use shapes that are congruent to
  this quadrilateral.

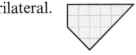

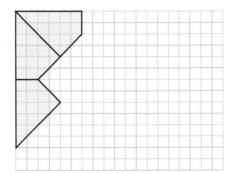

  b Use four of the quadrilaterals to make
  a tile that will tessellate.

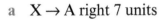

explanation 2a   explanation 2b

4 In the diagram, each shape may
be mapped to one other shape
by a translation.

Copy and complete the statements.

  a A → ☐   **b** ☐ → F
  c B → ☐   **d** ☐ → I
  e E → ☐   **f** ☐ → J

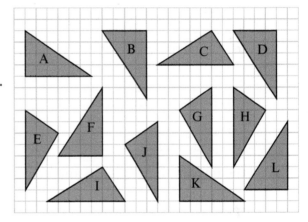

5 Copy this grid. Translate shape
X. Follow the instructions given
below.

Label the images A, B, C, D, E
and F.

  a X → A right 7 units

  b X → B right 4 units, up 2 units

  c X → C left 3 units, up 3 units

  d X → D down 6 units

  e X → E right 5 units, down
  7 units

  f X → F left 4 units, down
  2 units

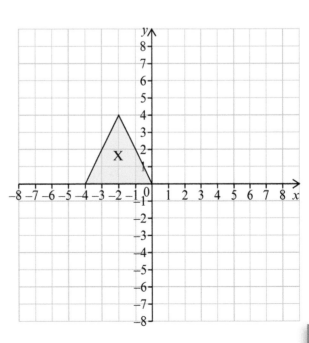

89

6 Describe each translation in question **5** using a column vector.

7 In each diagram, shape X has been translated to each of the shapes A, B, C, D, E and F. Describe each translation, using a column vector.

a

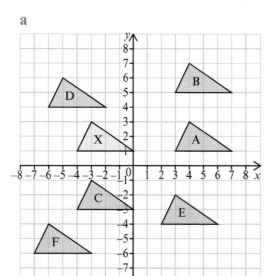

b

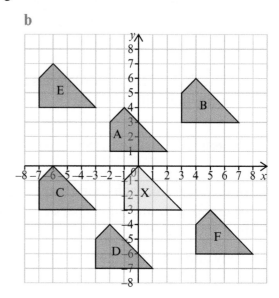

8 Copy this grid. Translate shape Y. Follow the instructions given below.

Label the images A, B, C, D, E and F.

a $Y \rightarrow A \begin{pmatrix} 3 \\ 4 \end{pmatrix}$

b $Y \rightarrow B \begin{pmatrix} -5 \\ 2 \end{pmatrix}$

c $Y \rightarrow C \begin{pmatrix} 2 \\ -7 \end{pmatrix}$

d $Y \rightarrow D \begin{pmatrix} -7 \\ 0 \end{pmatrix}$

e $Y \rightarrow E \begin{pmatrix} -4 \\ -5 \end{pmatrix}$

f $Y \rightarrow F \begin{pmatrix} 4 \\ -3 \end{pmatrix}$

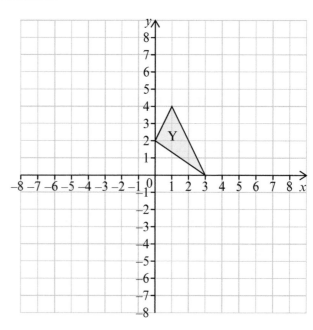

explanation 3a explanation 3b

9 Copy each diagram. Reflect each shape in the mirror line.

a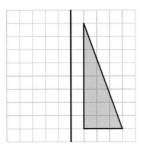
b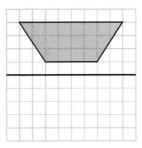
c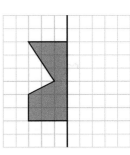

d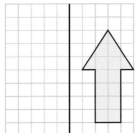
e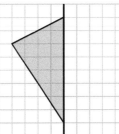
f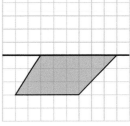

g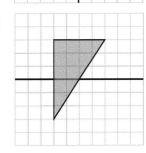
h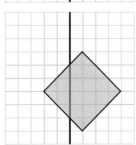
i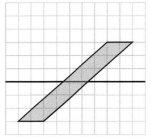

10 Copy each diagram. Reflect each shape in the diagonal mirror line.

a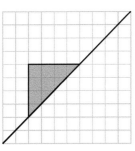
b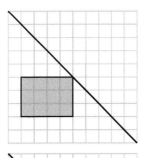
c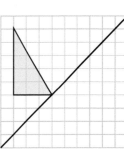

d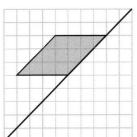
e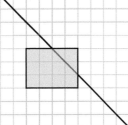
f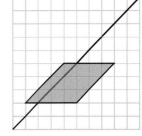

11 Copy each diagram. Draw in the missing mirror line.

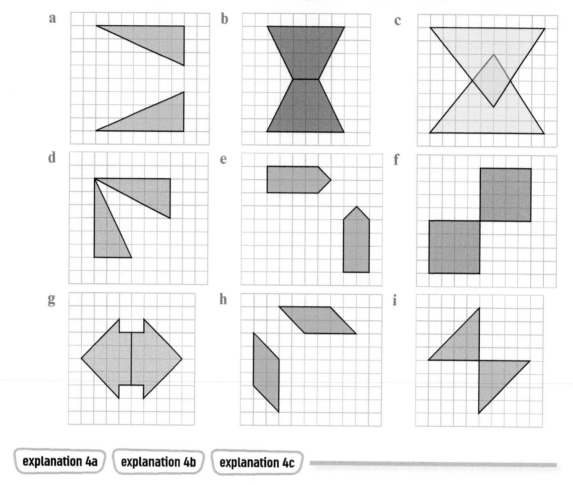

explanation 4a   explanation 4b   explanation 4c

12 Copy each diagram. Reflect each shape in the *y*-axis. Label each image A.

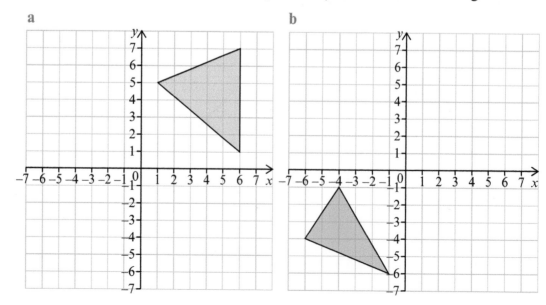

13 Use your diagrams from question **12**. Reflect the original shapes in the *x*-axis. Label each image **B**.

14 Copy each diagram. Reflect the shape in the dashed line.

a

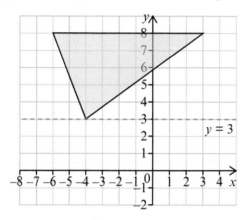

b

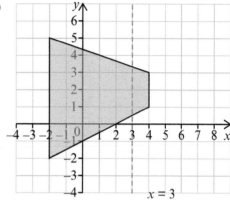

c

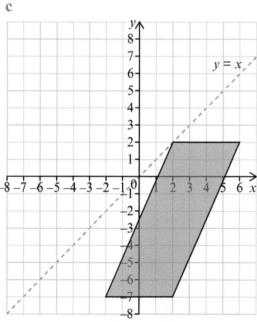

d

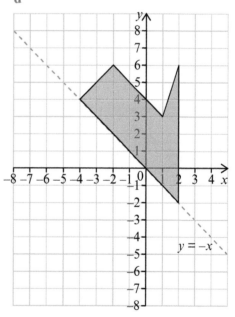

15 Shape A and shape B are reflections of shape X.

For each reflection, work out where the mirror line is.
Write its name or equation.

a

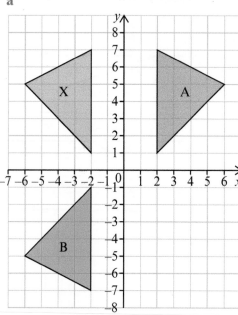

b

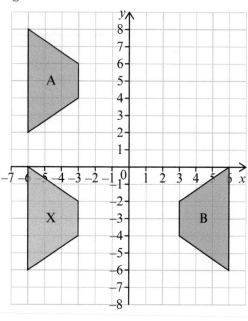

c

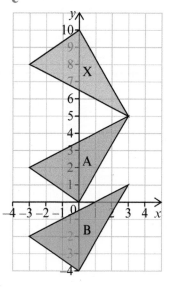

*d

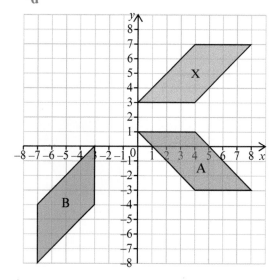

explanation 5a   explanation 5b

16 Copy each diagram. Show the new position of each shape after a clockwise rotation of 90° with each of these centres.

    i P   **ii** Q

a
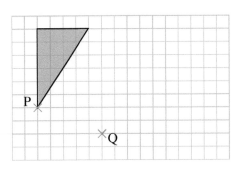

b
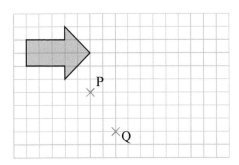

17 Copy each diagram. Show the new position of each shape after an anticlockwise rotation of 90° with each of these centres.

    i P   **ii** Q

a
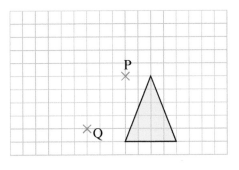

b
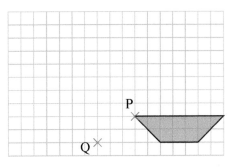

c
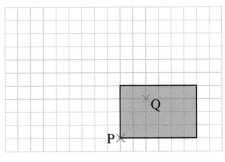

d
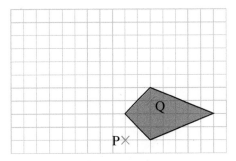

18 Copy each diagram. Show the new position of each shape after a rotation of 180° with each of these centres.

      i P   **ii** Q

a

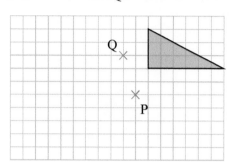

b

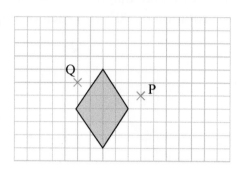

19 Look back at the diagrams in question **18**.

    a Explain why it isn't necessary to give the direction of rotation in question **18**.

    b Copy and complete this statement.

      A rotation of 90° anticlockwise is the same as a clockwise rotation of $\square°$.

20 Each diagram shows a rotation that moves shape **A** to shape **B**.

Decide which point is the centre of rotation and then describe the rotation.

(Remember to describe the angle, direction and centre.)

a

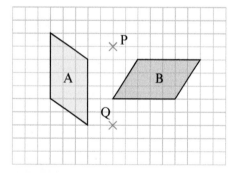

b

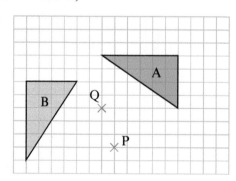

c

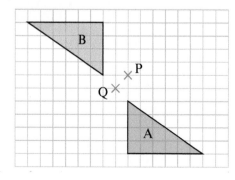

d

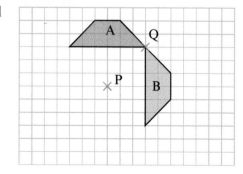

21 Copy each diagram. Rotate each shape using these instructions.

    i 90° clockwise about the origin. Label the image A.

    ii 180° about the origin. Label the image B.

    iii 90°anticlockwise about the point marked with the red cross. Label the image C.

a

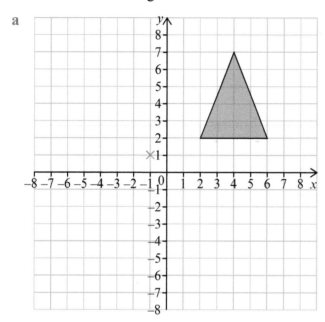

b

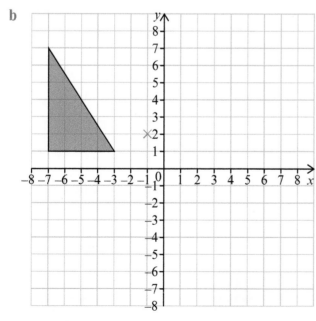

Enlargement

- Enlarging an object by a given scale factor
- Identifying enlargements and finding the scale factor of an enlargement
- Finding the centre of an enlargement
- Enlarging a shape, given a scale factor and a centre

Keywords

You should know

explanation 1a   explanation 1b

1 Copy each shape on squared paper. Enlarge each shape by scale factor 2.

a
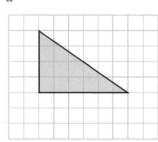

b
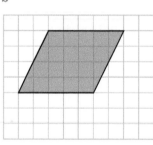

c
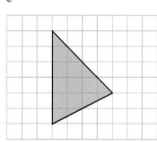

d
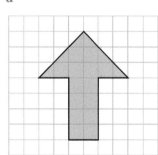

e
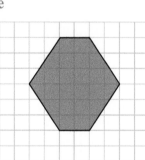

f
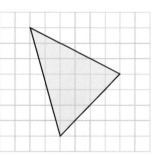

2 Copy each shape on squared paper. Enlarge each shape by scale factor 3.

a
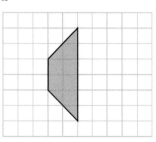

b
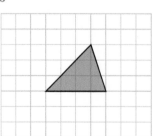

c
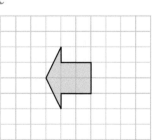

3 Copy each diagram. Enlarge each shape by the given scale factor.

a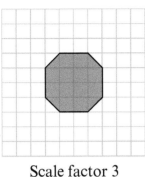

b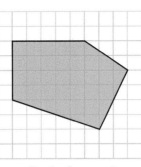

c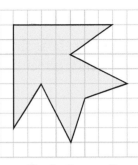

Scale factor 3   Scale factor 2   Scale factor 2

explanation 2

4 In each diagram, shape **B** is an enlargement of shape A.

What is the scale factor of each enlargement?

a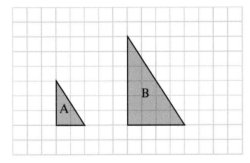

b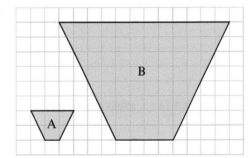

c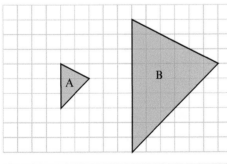

d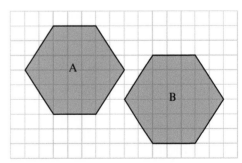

e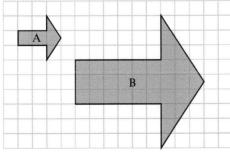

f

5 Look at the shapes in the diagram.

   a Which of the triangles are enlargements of triangle X?

   b For those shapes that are enlargements of X, state the scale factor of the enlargement.

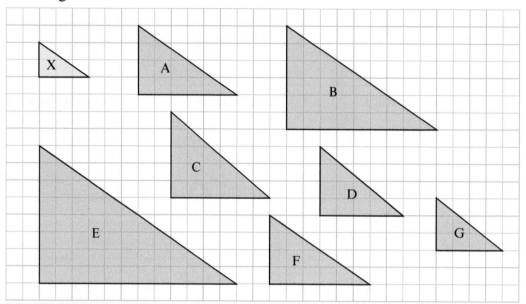

(explanation 3a)   (explanation 3b)

6 In each diagram, triangle B is an enlargement of triangle A by scale factor 2.

Copy each diagram. By drawing accurate rays, find the centre of each enlargement.

a

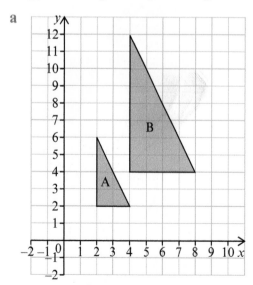

b

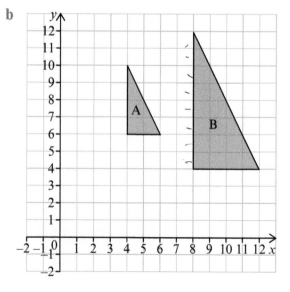

7 In each diagram, triangle B is an enlargement of triangle A by scale factor 2.

Copy each diagram. By drawing accurate rays, find the centre of each enlargement.

a

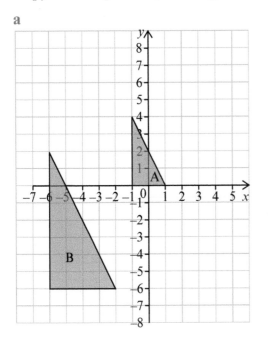

b

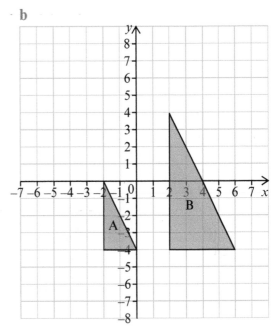

8 In each diagram, shape B is an enlargement of shape A by scale factor 2.

The centre of enlargement is inside shape A.

Copy each diagram. By drawing accurate rays, find the centre of each enlargement.

a

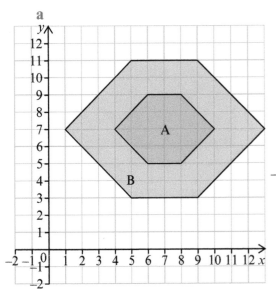

b

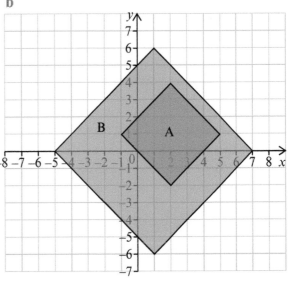

9 In each diagram, shape B is an enlargement of shape A.

    i Find the scale factor of each enlargement.

    ii Find the centre of each enlargement.

a

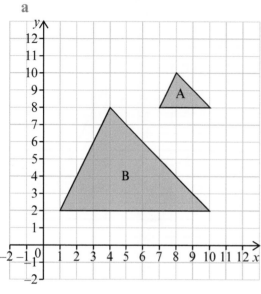

b

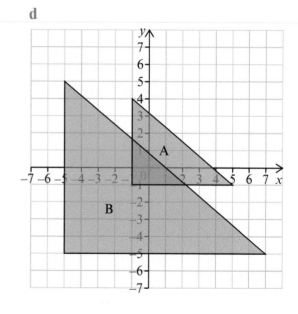

c

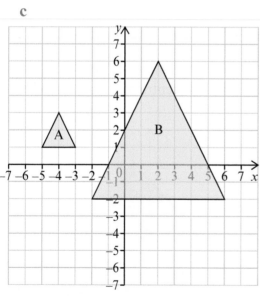

d

explanation 4a explanation 4b

10 Copy each diagram.

Enlarge each shape by scale factor 2 from the given centre of enlargement.
Use accurate rays.

a

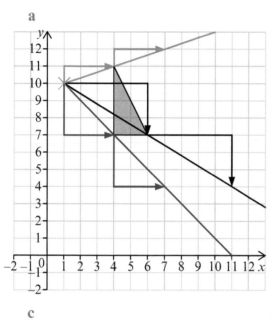

b

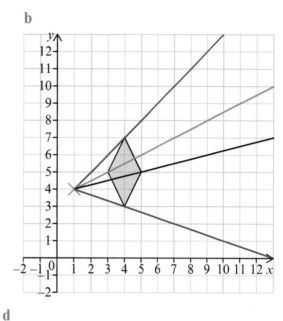

c

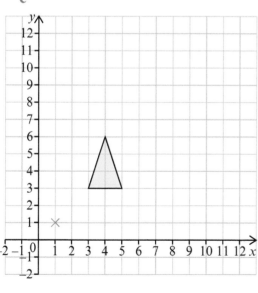

d

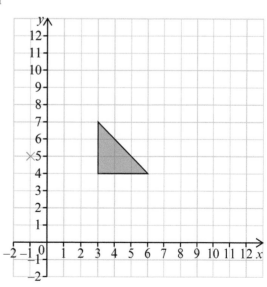

11 Copy each diagram.

Enlarge each shape by scale factor 3 from the given centre of enlargement.
Use accurate rays.

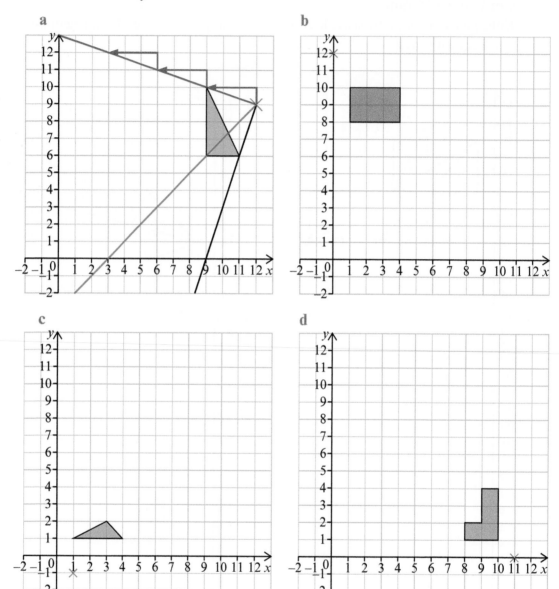

a

b

c

d

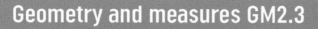

Geometry and measures GM2.3

Scale drawing

- Constructing triangles using a ruler and protractor or compasses
- Describing and measure three–figure bearings
- Interpreting diagrams drawn to scale
- Drawing diagrams to scale and using them to solve problems

Keywords

You should know

explanation 1a   explanation 1b   explanation 1c

1   Stephen is measuring an angle between two lines. He is using a 180° protractor. The diagram shows the angle that he is trying to measure.

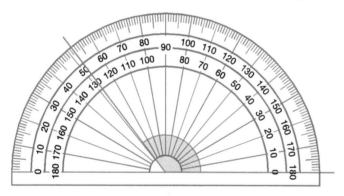

He thinks that the reading could be 132°, 128°, 52° or 68°.

a   How do you know that the angle can't be either 52° or 68°?

b   Which is the correct reading, 132° or 128°?

2   Find the *acute* angles shown on these protractor scales.

a    b    c    d

3 Find the *obtuse* angles shown on these protractor scales.

a  b  c  d

4 Find the angles shown on these 360° protractor scales.

a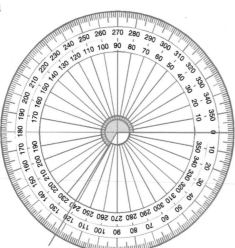

b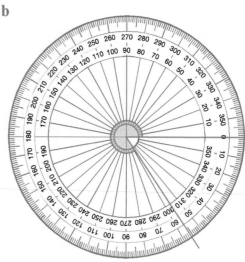

5 Use the information given on these diagrams to find the *reflex* angles.

a  b  c 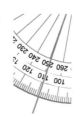 d

6 Use a protractor to draw these angles.

 a 45°   b 80°   c 132°   d 210°   e 327°

explanation 2a   explanation 2b   explanation 2c

7 The diagram shows the quadrilateral ABCD.

Write the size of these.

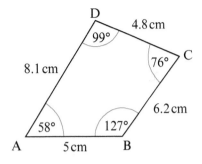

a AB

b DA

c BC

d CD

e ∠ABC

f ∠BCD

g ∠CDA

h ∠DAB

8 The sketch shows triangle ABC.

a Copy the sketch of the triangle.

b Add the measurements listed below to your sketch.

AB = 7 cm   ∠ABC = 70°

AC = 8 cm   ∠ACB = 53°

BC = 7.2 cm   ∠BAC = 57°

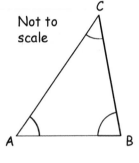

9 The sketch shows triangle XYZ.

a Use the information in this sketch to construct triangle XYZ.

b   i Measure YZ.

ii Measure angle XZY.

iii Measure angle XYZ.

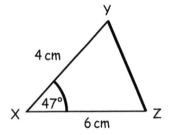

10 The sketch shows triangle RST.

a Use the information in this sketch to construct triangle RST.

b   i Measure RS.

ii Measure ∠TRS.

iii Measure ∠TSR.

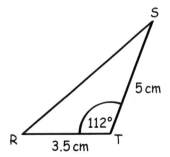

explanation 3a   explanation 3b   explanation 3c

11   The sketch shows triangle PQR.

   a   Use the information in this sketch to
     construct triangle PQR.

   b   i Measure PQ.   ii Measure QR.

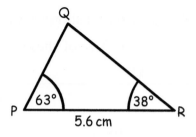

12   The sketch shows triangle UVW.

   a   Use the information in this sketch
     to construct triangle UVW.

   b   i Measure UW.

     ii Measure UV.

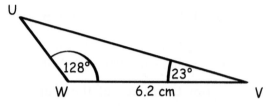

13   The diagram shows a map of an island. Team A lands at A. Team B lands at
    B. A and B are 8 km apart.

    The teams' meeting point, M,
    is positioned so that
    BAM is 65° and
    ABM is 35°.

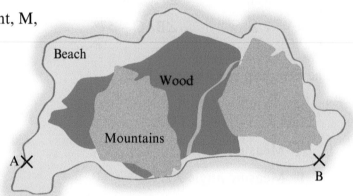

Scale
1 cm to 1 km

   a   Copy the diagram. Construct a triangle to find point M.

   b   Which team had to walk furthest to get to M? How much further was this?
     (Assume that the teams walk to the meeting point in straight lines.)

14   The sketch shows a scalene triangle.

   a   Use a ruler and a pair of compasses
     to construct the triangle.

   b   i Show that the angle PQR is 90°
       and mark this on your diagram.

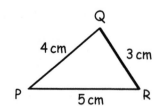

     ii What is the size of angle RPQ?

15 The sketch shows an isosceles triangle.

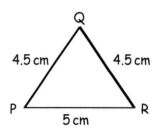

a Use a ruler and a pair of compasses to construct the triangle.

b i Show that the angle PRQ is 56° and mark this on your diagram.

ii What is the size of angle RQP?

16 The sketch shows an equilateral triangle.

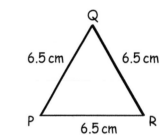

a Use a ruler and a pair of compasses to construct the triangle.

b What should each angle in the triangle measure? Why?

Measure the angles in the triangle to check the accuracy of your diagram.

17 The diagram shows triangle PQR.

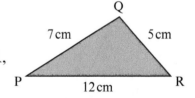

Explain why you can't construct the triangle PQR, where PR = 12 cm, PQ = 7 cm and QR = 5 cm.

18 The diagram shows the map of an island. Treasure is buried at a point Y on the island.

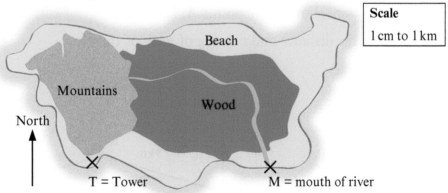

The treasure is 5.5 km from the tower and 4.5 km from the mouth of the river.

a Copy the diagram. Use a ruler and a pair of compasses to construct triangle TYM and find the treasure!

b Starting at the tower and facing north, what angle do you have to turn through to head for the treasure?

explanation 4a explanation 4b

19 Write the direction represented by each three-figure bearing.

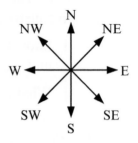

a 045°   b 180°

c 270°   d 315°

20 Write the three-figure bearing for each direction.

a North   b East   c South-east   d South-west

21 For each diagram, describe the distance and bearing of point B from point A.

a 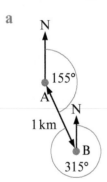   b 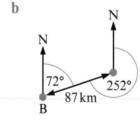   c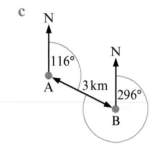

22 The diagram shows three points A, B and C.

What is the distance and bearing of each of these?

a B from A

b A from B

c B from C

d C from B

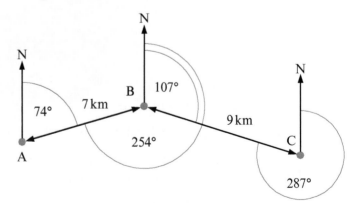

23 The diagram shows three points A, B and C.

Which points are these the distance and bearing of?

a 8 km on a bearing of 117°

b 8 km on a bearing of 297°

c 9 km on a bearing of 078°

d 9 km on a bearing of 258°

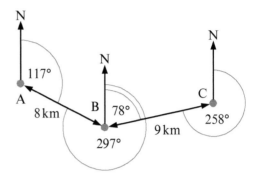

24 You need 5 mm squared paper. Plot points A, B and C as shown in the diagram.

B is 4 squares below and 8 squares to the right of A.

C is 6 squares to the right and 8 squares above B.

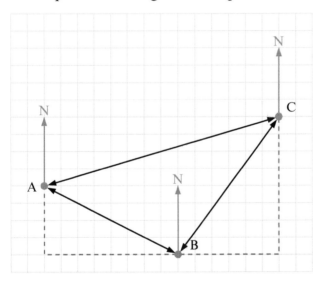

a Measure the line AB, giving your answer to the nearest millimetre.

b Measure the bearing of B from A.

c What is the distance and bearing of C from B?

d What is the distance and bearing of A from C?

25 You need 5 mm squared paper. Plot points A, B and C as shown in the diagram.

B is 5 squares above and
6 squares to the right of A.

C is 3 squares below and
14 squares to the right of A.

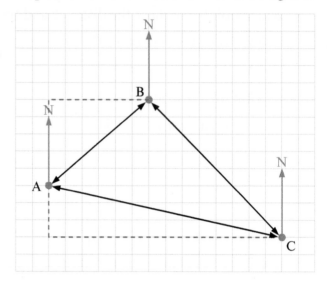

a   What is the distance and bearing of B from A?

b   What is the distance and bearing of C from A?

c   What is the distance and bearing of B from C?

| explanation 5a | explanation 5b | explanation 5c |

26 The diagram shows two points A and B.

The bearing of B from A is 130°.

a   Explain why the angle marked x is 130°

b   Explain why the angle marked y is 180°.

c   What is the distance and bearing of A from B?

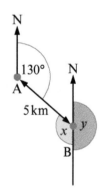

27 The diagram shows two points A and B.

The bearing of B from A is 120°.

a   Explain why the angle marked x is 60°

b   Explain why the angle marked y is 300°.

c   What is the distance and bearing of A from B?

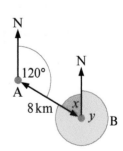

28 For each diagram below, work out the distance and bearing of point A from point B.

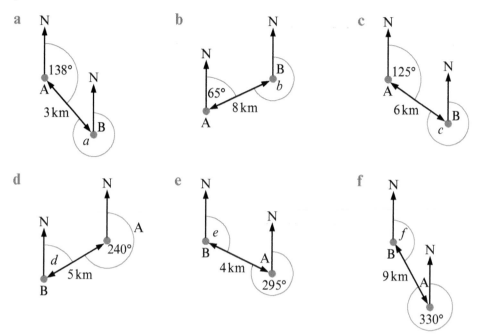

a   138°   A   3 km   B   N   N   a

b   N   B   b   65°   8 km   A   N

c   N   125°   A   6 km   B   N   c

d   N   N   A   240°   d   5 km   B

e   N   N   e   B   4 km   A   295°

f   N   f   B   N   9 km   A   330°

29 The bearing from Bedford to Norwich is 065°.
What is the bearing of Bedford from Norwich?

> **explanation 6**

30 The diagram shows part of a map of the UK.

The map uses the scale 1 cm to 10 km.

a   Work out the distance in kilometres between these.

    i   York and Scarborough

    ii York and Beverley

b   The distance between York and Darlington is 68 km.

    What would be the distance shown on the map?

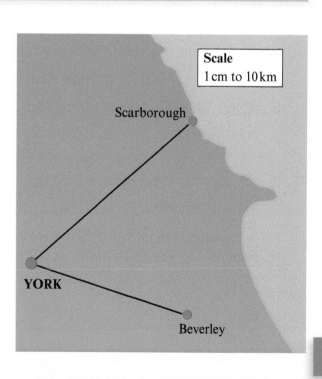

Scale
1 cm to 10 km

Scarborough

YORK

Beverley

31 The diagram shows part of a road map of the UK.

The scale on the map is 1 cm to 20 km.

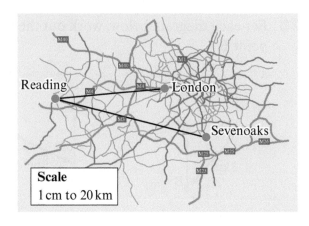

a Work out the distance in kilometres between these places.

   i London and Reading

   ii Reading and Sevenoaks

b The distance between Sevenoaks and Cambridge is approximately 114 km.

What would the distance be between Sevenoaks and Cambridge on the map?

32 The scale on a map is 1 cm to 5 km.

a What are the actual distances for these measurements on the map?

   i 3 cm   **ii** 8 cm   **iii** 0.5 cm   **iv** 3.5 cm   **v** 0.25 cm

b What would be the measurements on the map for these actual distances?

   i 25 km   **ii** 45 km   **iii** 10 km   **iv** 1 km   **v** 1.5 km

> **explanation 7**

33 Write each scale as a ratio. Write your ratio in its simplest form.

   a 1 cm : 1 m   **b** 1 cm : 4 m   **c** 50 cm : 2 m

   d 60 cm : 3 m   **e** 1 cm : 1 km   **f** 1 cm : 2 km

   g 2 cm : 1 km   **h** 5 cm : 1 km   **i** 4 cm : 5 km

34 A scale drawing uses the scale 8 cm to 1 km.

a Explain why the scale is 12 500.

b A measurement on the drawing is 5 cm.
Explain why the real distance is 625 m.

35 A map of the UK shows the distance between Birmingham and Nottingham as 3.5 cm.

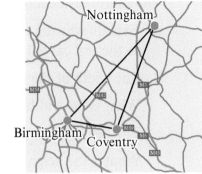

   a The distance between Birmingham and Nottingham is approximately 70 km.

      Work out the scale on the map.
Write it in the form 1 cm to ☐.

   b On the map Birmingham and Coventry are 1.4 cm apart.

      Work out the distance in kilometres between Birmingham and Coventry.

36 The plans of a house were drawn to scale. The scale was 4 cm to 1 m.

   a The length of the kitchen is 3.5 m.
What is the length of the kitchen on the plans?

   b On the plans, the width of the kitchen is 6 cm.
What is the width of the real kitchen?

   c Write the scale as a ratio.

37 A city centre map is drawn with a scale of 1 : 5000.

   a Write the map scale as 1 cm to ☐ m

   b The distance from the theatre to the library is shown as 3.8 cm along the main road.

      What is the real distance?

   c The distance between the theatre and the museum is 335 m.

      What distance would be shown in centimetres on the map?

38 The length of a car is 4 m 80 cm. Mr Jones made a model of the car.

The length of the model is 40 cm.

a   Explain why the scale of the model to the real car is 1 : 12.

b   The width of the model is 18 cm.

What is the width of the real car?

c   The height of the car is 1 m 32 cm.

What is the height of the model?

39 The diagram shows the plan of a one-bedroom ground floor flat but it is not drawn to scale.

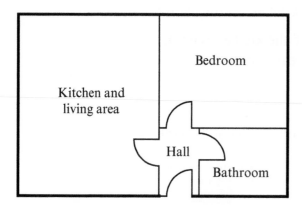

a   Using the measurements below and a scale of 1 : 60, draw a scale drawing of the flat.

Kitchen and living area = 5.4 m × 3.6 m

Bedroom = 3 m × 3 m

Bathroom = 2.40 m × 1.80 m

b   What are the dimensions of the hall?

40 A football pitch has dimensions as shown.

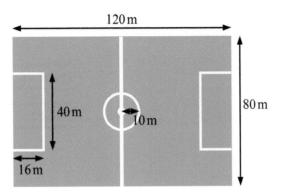

a　Draw a scale diagram of the football pitch. Use a scale of 1 cm to 8 m.

b　Write the scale of the drawing as a ratio.

41 Sheffield is 120 km from Blackpool on a bearing of 115°.

Stoke-on-Trent is 100 km from Blackpool on a bearing of 145°.

Use a scale of 1 cm to 20 km.

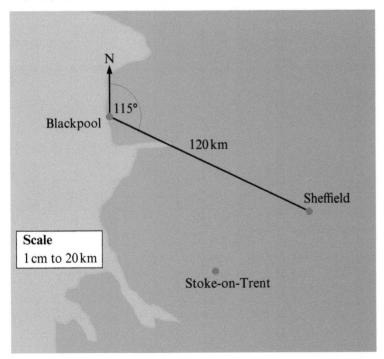

a　Draw a scale diagram to show the positions of Blackpool, Sheffield and Stoke-on-Trent.

b　Use your diagram to work out the distance and bearing of Sheffield from Stoke-on-Trent.

Forming and solving equations

- Forming and solving equations
- Solving problems using algebra

Keywords

You should know

explanation 1

1 Solve these equations by using inverse operations.

Use substitution to check your answers.

a $2p - 3 = 11$

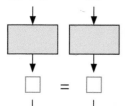

$2p = \square$

$p = \square$

b $5q + 11 = 26$

$\square = \square$

$q = \square$

c $3r - 1 = 8$

$\square = \square$

$r = \square$

d $6t + 8 = 50$

$\square = \square$

$t = \square$

e $3g - 7 = 17$

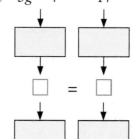

$\square = \square$

$g = \square$

f $8m + 5 = 29$

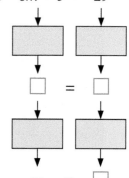

$\square = \square$

$m = \square$

explanation 2

2 Solve these equations by using inverse operations.
Use substitution to check your answers.

a $\dfrac{p}{2} + 3 = 11$

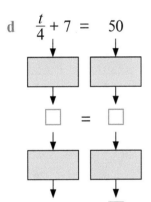

$\dfrac{p}{2} = \square$

$p = \square$

b $\dfrac{q}{3} + 5 = 9$

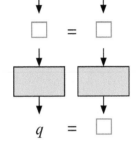

$\square = \square$

$q = \square$

c $\dfrac{r}{2} - 1 = 9$

$\square = \square$

$r = \square$

d $\dfrac{t}{4} + 7 = 50$

$\square = \square$

$t = \square$

e $\dfrac{g}{3} - 4 = 17$

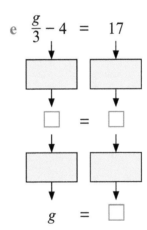

$\square = \square$

$g = \square$

f $\dfrac{m}{5} + 3 = 7$

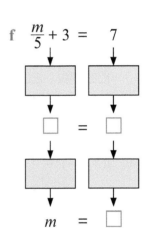

$\square = \square$

$m = \square$

3 Solve these equations by using inverse operations.
Remember to check your answers by substitution.

a $3x - 4 = 26$

b $8t + 6 = 30$

c $5p - 6 = 34$

d $3w + 12 = 30$

e $5r - 10 = 25$

f $\dfrac{t}{2} + 8 = 10$

g $3d + 18 = 24$

h $\dfrac{y}{3} - 2 = 4$

i $3e - 4 = 23$

j $\dfrac{b}{4} - 2 = 9$

k $2f + 4 = 19$

l $2g - 8 = 40$

m $5x - 4 = 26$

n $\dfrac{t}{2} - 2 = 5$

o $6w - 12 = 18$

explanation 3

4 Expand the brackets in these expressions.

- **a** $3(x + 2)$
- **b** $4(n - 6)$
- **c** $7(t + 1)$
- **d** $9(h - 4)$
- **e** $5(p + 10)$
- **f** $4(b - 2)$
- **g** $8(x - 3)$
- **h** $12(n - 4)$
- **i** $6(t + 5)$

5 Copy and complete these. Check your answers by using substitution.

a $2(x + 3) = 20$

$2x + 6 = 20$

$2x = \square$

$x = \square$

b $3(x + 1) = 12$

$\square = 12$

$\square = \square$

$x = \square$

c $2(x - 6) = 24$

$\square = 24$

$\square = \square$

$x = \square$

d $2(x + 4) = 30$

$\square = \square$

$\square = \square$

$x = \square$

e $3(x - 4) = 18$

$\square = \square$

$\square = \square$

$x = \square$

f $5(x + 2) = 25$

$\square = \square$

$\square = \square$

$x = \square$

6 Solve these equations.

a $2(x + 5) = 18$

b $8(t - 7) = 32$

c $3(m + 5) = 15$

d $4(n - 10) = 24$

e $7(p - 3) = 21$

f $9(y - 6) = 45$

g $6(f - 5) = 18$

h $9(a - 6) = 36$

i $4(x - 12) = 8$

j $4(3p + 1) = 28$

k $3(3q - 2) = 30$

l $3(2w - 4) = 18$

explanation 4a   explanation 4b

7 Simplify these expressions by collecting like terms.

a $y + 3 + 2y + 5$

b $2 + 3x + 5x$

c $2x + 5x + x + 3$

d $c + 2 + 4c - 3$

e $3p + 8 + 2p$

f $5 + 3x + 4x - 3$

g $5x + 6 - x - 3$

h $5y + 7 - y - 4$

i $6y - 3 - 2y + 4$

j $3p + 4 + 2p - 7$

k $3s + 6 + 4s - 2$

l $8m + 6 - 3m + 4$

8 This question is about the equation $4x - 1 + x + 7 = 41$.

a Explain why the equation $4x - 1 + x + 7 = 41$ simplifies to $5x + 6 = 41$.

b Solve the equation by using inverse operations.

c Substitute your answer into the equation to check that it is correct.

9 This question is about the equation $3x - 4 + x - 1 = 35$.

a Explain why the equation $3x - 4 + x - 1 = 35$ simplifies to $4x - 5 = 35$.

b Solve the equation by using inverse operations.

c Substitute your answer into the equation to check that it is correct.

10 This question is about the equation $5x + 3 - 2x - 7 = 11$.

a Explain why the equation $5x + 3 - 2x - 7 = 11$ simplifies to $3x - 4 = 11$.

b Solve the equation by using inverse operations.

c Substitute your answer into the equation to check that it is correct.

11 Simplify the equations first. Then solve them by using inverse operations.

a $2x + 5 + x + 1 = 24$ b $3r + 5 + 2r + 1 = 26$

c $2p + 6p - 3 = 37$ d $4w - 12 + 6w - 8 = 60$

e $8t + 6 - 3t - 1 = 35$ f $5g + 4 - 2g + 3 = 19$

g $7d - 2 - 3d - 2 = 28$ h $5y - 3 - 3y - 1 = 6$

i $3e - 5 + 2e - 2 = 18$ j $5b - 6 + 2b - 7 = 8$

> explanation 5a   explanation 5b

12 The perimeter of the triangle shown is 44 cm.

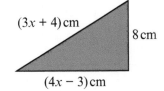

a Show that this information gives the equation $7x + 9 = 44$.

b Solve the equation.

c What are the lengths of the three sides of the triangle?

13 The perimeter of the rectangle shown is 40 cm.

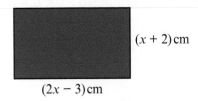

a Show that this information gives the equation $6x - 2 = 40$.

b Solve the equation.

c Find the length of the longer side of the rectangle.

14 The perimeter of the square shown is 28 cm.

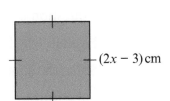

a Show that this information gives the equation $4(2x - 3) = 28$.

b Solve the equation to find x.

c What is the side length of the square?

*15 For each shape, form an equation for the perimeter and solve it.

Use your answer to find the length of each of the sides.

a

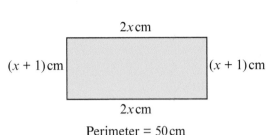

2x cm

(x + 1) cm   (x + 1) cm

2x cm

Perimeter = 50 cm

b

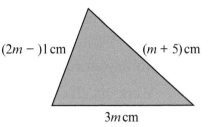

(2m −)1 cm   (m + 5) cm

3m cm

Perimeter = 40 cm

16 The diagram shows two angles around a point.

a Explain why 3x + 50 + x + 30 = 360.

b Simplify the equation from part **a**.

c Solve the equation to find x.

d Find the two angles around the point.

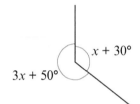

x + 30°

3x + 50°

*17 The sum of the angles in any triangle is 180°.

Use this to write an equation for each diagram and then solve the equation.

a

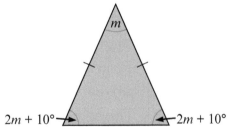

m

2m + 10°   2m + 10°

b

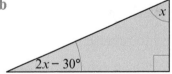

x

2x − 30°

18 This is an addition pyramid.

a Copy and complete the pyramid. Write each expression as simply as possible.

b The number at the top is 13. Write an equation involving x.

c Solve your equation to find x.

d Work out all of the values in the pyramid. Use them to check that your value of x is correct.

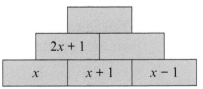

2x + 1

x   x + 1   x − 1

19 **a** Copy and complete this addition pyramid.

b The value at the top of the pyramid is 46.

Use this fact to write an equation involving x.

c Solve your equation to find x.

d Work out all of the values in the pyramid. Use them to check that your value of x is correct.

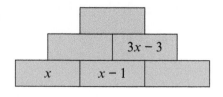

20 **a** Copy and complete this addition pyramid.

b All of the blocks in the pyramid add up to 47.

Use this fact to write an equation involving x.

c Solve your equation to find x.

d Work out all of the values in the pyramid. Use them to check that your value of x is correct.

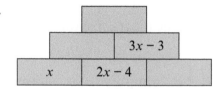

21 You can use algebra to help you solve the puzzle shown on the scroll.

Use x to represent Polly's age in years.

a Write an expression for Amy's age, using x.

b Write an expression for James' age, using x.

c Write an expression for the sum of all three ages. Simplify it.

d Write an equation. Use the fact that their ages add to 26.

e Solve the equation.

f How old is each child?

Amy is 5 years older than her sister Polly. Polly is 3 years older than her brother James. The sum of the three children's ages is 26. How old are the three children?

Equations and formulae

- Using formulae to solve problems

explanation 1

1 Copy and complete these. Check your answers by using substitution.

a $\quad 2x + 5 = 23$

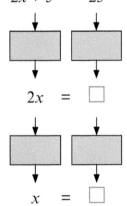

$2x = \square$

$x = \square$

b $\quad 23 = 4x - 9$

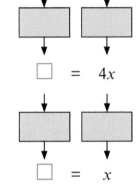

$\square = 4x$

$\square = x$

c $\quad 3 = \dfrac{x}{2} - 8$

$\square = \dfrac{x}{2}$

$\square = x$

d $\quad 32 = 2x - 10$

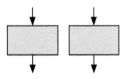

$\square = 2x$

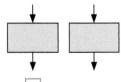

$\square = x$

e $\quad 27 = 4x + 3$

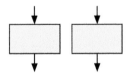

$\square = 4x$

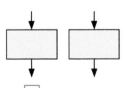

$\square = x$

f $\quad 10 = \dfrac{x}{2} + 7$

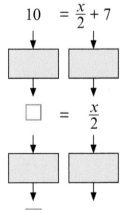

$\square = \dfrac{x}{2}$

$\square = x$

2 Solve these equations. Check your answers by using substitution.

a $6x - 10 = 14$ b $8x - 12 = 20$ c $\frac{x}{2} + 6 = 14$

d $32 = 9g - 4$ e $12 = \frac{p}{3} + 2$ f $5x + 9 = 14$

g $6t - 12 = 12$ h $30 = 9h + 12$ i $\frac{q}{2} - 8 = 12$

*j $12 = 4y + 10$ *k $12 = 3n + 15$ *l $\frac{t}{2} + 9 = 8$

---

explanation 2

3 Copy and complete these. Check your answers by using substitution.

a $4(x + 3) = \quad 20$

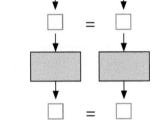

b $35 \quad = 5(x - 1)$

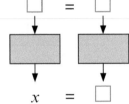

c $24 \quad = 3(x + 6)$

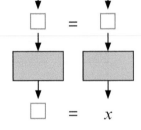

d $18 \quad = 2(x + 6)$

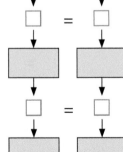

e $24 \quad = 2(x - 5)$

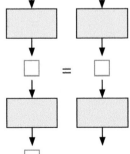

f $28 \quad = 4(x + 3)$

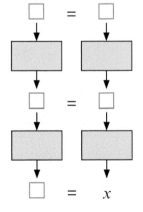

4 Solve these equations. Check your answers by using substitution.

a $3x + 6 = 30$

b $12 = \frac{x}{3} + 2$

c $7x - 4 = 24$

d $6(x - 2) = 30$

e $21 = 3(x - 9)$

f $2(x + 6) = 28$

g $\frac{x}{3} - 8 = 15$

h $18 = 2(x - 8)$

i $24 = 3(x + 5)$

(explanation 3a) (explanation 3b)

5 Sian downloads 10 songs from the internet. Each song costs £C. Sian spends £T.

She writes this formula for her spending:

$T = 10C$

a   Each song cost £0.79. How much would 10 songs cost?

b   By buying 10 songs, Sian got a discount and spent a total of £6.50. Work out the cost of each song.

6 Simon is buying a new sofa that costs £T.

He plans to put down a deposit of £200 and pay the rest off in 12 monthly instalments of £M.

He uses this formula:

$T = 200 + 12M$

a   Simon pays £50 per month. How much would the sofa cost altogether?

b   If the sofa was in the sale and was reduced to £500, how much would Simon have to pay each month?

7 Caroline is working on her maths homework.

This matchstick pattern has the formula:

$M = 3S + 1$

M = total number of matchsticks and S = number of squares made.

a How many matchsticks are needed to make 10 squares?

b Caroline has 40 matchsticks. How many squares can she make?

c Explain why you can't use 80 matchsticks to make a term in this pattern.

8 Richard and his friends want to go to the cinema.

It will cost Richard £C for a cinema ticket and £B for the return bus fare. The total cost is £T.

He writes this formula:

$T = C + B$

a A cinema ticket costs £4.50 and the return bus ticket is £2.75.

How much money will Richard need to go to the cinema?

b Richard and his friends went to an early showing of the film as the cinema tickets were cheaper.

He spent £6.50 altogether.

How much did his cinema ticket cost?

9 Rachel is making a roast chicken dinner.
The cooking time for the chicken is 20 minutes per pound plus 15 minutes.

She uses this formula:

$T = 20P + 15$

T = total time in minutes
P = number of pounds (lbs) in weight

a   How long should she cook a chicken for if it weighs 6 lbs?
Give your answer in hours and minutes.

b   The label on a pre-packed chicken says that it should be cooked for 1 hour
and 45 minutes.

  i   How many minutes is this?

  ii   How much must the chicken weigh in pounds?

10 Tim wants to convert temperatures between
degrees Fahrenheit (°F) and degrees
Celsius (°C) for his science project.

He uses this formula:

$F = 1.8C + 32$

F = temperature in °F
C = temperature in °C

a   Water freezes at 0°C.

What temperature is this in °F?

b   Tim recorded the temperature on a summer day as 77°F.

What temperature is this in °C?

c   In the winter the coldest temperature Tim measured was 23°F.

What temperature is this in °C?

11 Mrs Jones and her three children are going to the zoo.

An adult ticket costs £A and a child ticket costs £C.

Altogether the tickets cost £T.

Mrs Jones writes the formula $T = A + 3C$.

a   If an adult ticket costs £12 and a child ticket costs £8, then what was the total cost of the tickets?

b   If the tickets cost £45 altogether and a child ticket was £10, then how much was an adult ticket?

c   If the tickets cost £40 altogether and an adult ticket was £13, then how much was a child ticket?

12 Michael uses this formula to work out his monthly phone bill:

$T = L + 0.05M$

T = total cost
L = cost of line rental
M = number of minutes spent on making calls

The cost of a call is 5p or £0.05 per minute.

a   How many minutes are in 5 hours?

b   What is the total cost of Michael's phone bill if the line rental costs £12 and his call time is 5 hours?

c   The phone company reduced the line rental. Michael's next bill was £18.

His call time was 4 hours altogether.

What was the new cost of the line rental?

Solving equations (2)

- Solving equations where the unknown term is subtracted
- Solving equations with the unknown on both sides

Keywords

You should know

explanation 1

1 Copy and complete these. Check your answers by using substitution.

a $12 - x = 2$

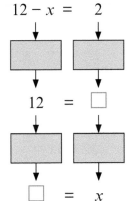

$12 = \square$

$\square = x$

b $18 - x = 11$

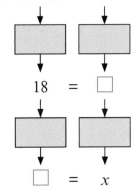

$18 = \square$

$\square = x$

c $10 - x = 15$

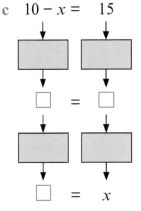

$\square = \square$

$\square = x$

d $18 - x = 5$

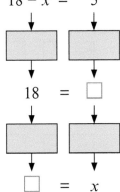

$18 = \square$

$\square = x$

e $36 - x = 17$

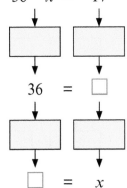

$36 = \square$

$\square = x$

f $12 - x = 21$

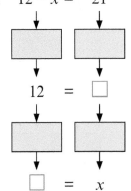

$12 = \square$

$\square = x$

2 Solve these equations. Check your answers by using substitution.

a $28 - x = 9$

b $17 - x = 12$

c $10 - t = 3$

d $g + 5 = 19$

e $p - 8 = 10$

f $12 - x = 9$

g $5 + x = 17$

h $16 - h = 7$

i $4 + q = 17$

*j $12 + g = 8$

*k $12 - t = 23$

*l $5 - d = 8$

explanation 2a explanation 2b

3 Copy and complete these. Check your answers by using substitution.

a $15 - 2x = 3$

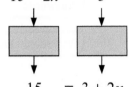

$15 = 3 + 2x$

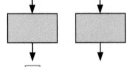

$\square = 2x$

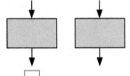

$\square = x$

b $24 - 3x = 9$

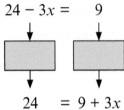

$24 = 9 + 3x$

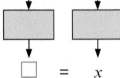

$\square = 3x$

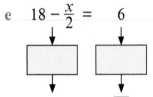

$\square = x$

c $36 - 4x = 8$

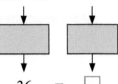

$36 = \square$

$\square = \square$

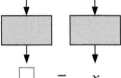

$\square = x$

d $12 - \dfrac{x}{3} = 10$

$12 = \square$

$\square = \square$

$\square = x$

e $18 - \dfrac{x}{2} = 6$

$18 = \square$

$\square = \square$

$\square = x$

f $32 - 5x = -3$

$32 = \square$

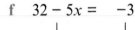

$\square = \square$

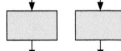

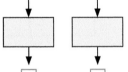

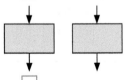

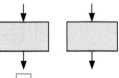

$\square = x$

4 Solve these equations. Check your answers by using substitution.

a $23 - 2x = 9$ b $45 - 3x = 12$ c $30 - 4t = 2$

d $19 - 3g = 4$ e $24 - p = 18$ f $29 - 3x = 11$

g $15 - x = 7$ h $15 - 2h = 9$ i $48 - 5q = 13$

*j $12 - g = 17$ *k $12 - 3t = 15$ *l $5 - 3d = 17$

5 Solve the following equations. Check your answers by using substitution.

a $6x - 15 = 9$ b $15 - 2x = 3$ c $18 - t = 6$

d $18 = 2g + 4$ e $\frac{p}{2} = 32$ f $12 = 10 + 2x$

g $8g - 3 = 29$ h $13 = 25 - 6q$ i $10 - \frac{q}{2} = 6$

j $2y + 12 = 28$ k $3n - 14 = 22$ l $\frac{t}{2} + 9 = 21$

m $\frac{x}{3} - 6 = 14$ n $8 = \frac{d}{4} + 5$ o $8 = 12 - 4x$

*6 Solve the following equations. Check your answers by using substitution.

a $12x - 6 = 30$ b $18 = 3(x - 1)$ c $12 = 3(x - 4)$

d $24 = 2(x - 3)$ e $14 - 2x = 8$ f $21 = 3 - x$

g $28 = 4(x - 1)$ h $3 = \frac{x}{4} - 8$ i $5 - \frac{x}{3} = 2$

j $25 = 7 - 3x$ k $5(x - 3) = 45$ l $3(4 - x) = 18$

m $\frac{x}{5} - 6 = 4$ n $7 = \frac{d}{4} + 3$ o $18 = 12 - 3x$

7 a   Copy and complete this addition pyramid to show that the term at the top is $20 - 4x$.

b   If the term at the top is equal to 8, write an equation involving x.

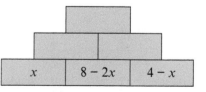

c   Solve your equation to find x.

d   Work out all the values in the pyramid and use them to check your value of x is correct.

explanation 3

8   Copy and complete these. Check your answers by using substitution.

a $3x + 2 = x + 8$

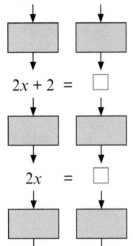

$2x + 2 = \square$

$2x = \square$

$x = \square$

b $4x - 3 = x + 6$

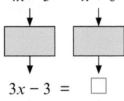

$3x - 3 = \square$

$3x = \square$

$x = \square$

c $6x + 3 = 4x + 7$

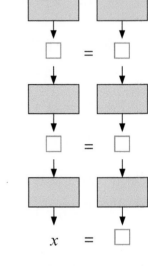

$\square = \square$

$\square = \square$

$x = \square$

d $4x - 3 = x + 9$

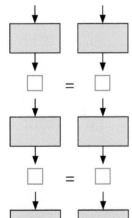

$\square = \square$

$\square = \square$

$x = \square$

e $6x - 2 = 4x + 8$

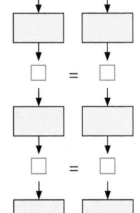

$\square = \square$

$\square = \square$

$x = \square$

f $x + 6 = 5x + 2$

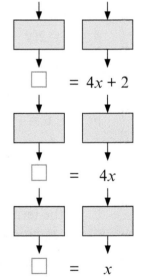

$\square = 4x + 2$

$\square = 4x$

$\square = x$

9   Solve the following equations. Check your answers by using substitution.

a $6x + 8 = 3x + 20$

b $3x + 6 = x + 18$

c $6x - 4 = 2x + 4$

d $7p + 5 = 2p + 45$

e $3n + 4 = n + 12$

f $5m + 1 = 2m + 7$

g $6f - 9 = f + 1$

h $2y + 15 = 4y + 9$

i $k + 12 = 5k + 8$

10 Solve the following equations. Check your answers by using substitution.

a $9x + 1 = 5x + 21$ b $3m - 6 = 2m + 7$ c $4k - 5 = 3k - 1$

d $5x + 5 = 3x - 7$ e $12x - 3 = x + 8$ f $6x - 2 = 2x - 10$

*g $10x + 12 = 8x$ *h $7u - 4 = 9u + 6$ *i $5 + r = 8r - 9$

explanation 4

*11 Copy and complete these. Check your answers by using substitution.

a $3x - 5 = 10 - 2x$ b $6x - 2 = 14 - 2x$ c $4 - x = 5x - 8$

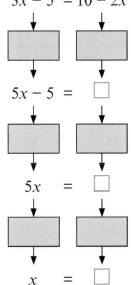
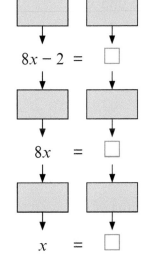
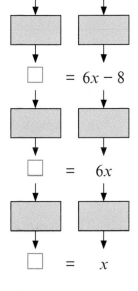

d $4x - 4 = 10 - 3x$ e $7x - 4 = 16 - 3x$ f $6 - 2x = 3x - 9$

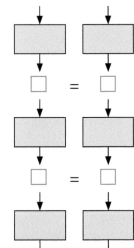
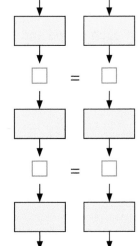
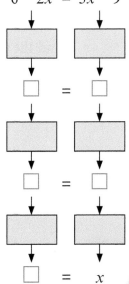

135

*12 Solve the following equations. Check your answers by using substitution.

a $4x - 8 = 13 - 3x$ b $3x - 6 = 4x - 10$ c $6x - 14 = 10 - 2x$

d $5 - 2b = 3b + 25$ e $7 + 3y = 5y - 2$ f $4m + 7 = 8m + 5$

g $9 - 3q = 5q + 1$ h $25 - 2y = 2y + 5$ i $6 - 2q = 3q - 9$

j $9x - 4 = 24 - 5x$ k $2m - 3 = 3m - 7$ l $18 - 4x = 12 - 2x$

13 The diagram shows a square with the length of its sides written using algebra.

a Explain why $2x + 3 = 3x - 2$.

b Solve the equation to find x.

c What is the side length of the square?

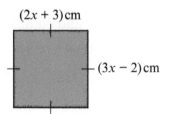

$(2x + 3)$ cm

$(3x - 2)$ cm

14 The sketch shows an isosceles triangle.

a Explain why $4x + 15° = 2x + 45°$.

b Solve the equation to find x.

c Find the three angles in the triangle.

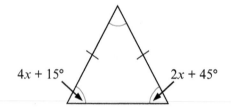

$4x + 15°$ $2x + 45°$

*15 The square has side lengths of $(2x + 2)$ cm.
The equilateral triangle has side lengths of $(10 - x)$ cm.
Their perimeters are equal.

a Explain why $8x + 8 = 30 - 3x$.

b Solve the equation to find x.

c Find the perimeter of each shape and check that they are equal.

$(2x + 2)$ cm

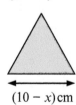

$(10 - x)$ cm

Using fractions and percentages

- Ordering fractions
- Converting percentages to fractions
- Converting fractions to percentages
- Finding a percentage of an amount
- Finding one number as a percentage of another
- Increasing and decreasing an amount by a percentage
- Finding the increase or decrease as a percentage

Keywords

You should know

explanation 1a   explanation 1b   explanation 1c

1 **i** Write each pair of fractions with a common denominator.

ii Copy and complete each statement by writing < or > instead of the box.

a $\frac{1}{4} \square \frac{1}{3}$ b $\frac{5}{6} \square \frac{3}{4}$ c $\frac{2}{3} \square \frac{5}{8}$ d $\frac{9}{5} \square \frac{4}{3}$

e $\frac{2}{9} \square \frac{1}{4}$ f $\frac{5}{8} \square \frac{4}{6}$ g $\frac{5}{3} \square \frac{10}{7}$ h $\frac{7}{12} \square \frac{3}{5}$

> < means 'is smaller than'.
> > means 'is bigger than'.

2 Use equivalent fractions to find the smaller fraction in each pair.

a $\frac{3}{4}, \frac{5}{12}$ b $\frac{2}{3}, \frac{5}{6}$ c $\frac{5}{6}, \frac{4}{5}$ d $\frac{2}{3}, \frac{12}{21}$ e $\frac{2}{5}, \frac{1}{2}$ f $\frac{5}{8}, \frac{2}{3}$

3 Write the pairs of fractions in question **1** as decimals.

Use them to check your answers to the question.

4 Change the fractions to decimals to put these fractions in order from smallest to largest.

a $\frac{2}{3}, \frac{3}{4}$ b $\frac{3}{8}, \frac{4}{7}$ c $\frac{11}{12}, \frac{4}{5}$

d $\frac{11}{15}, \frac{14}{20}$ e $\frac{1}{4}, \frac{3}{10}, \frac{1}{5}$ f $\frac{2}{5}, \frac{7}{20}, \frac{3}{8}$

5 Brendon, Kieran and Peter were all given identical pizzas.

Brendon ate $\frac{3}{10}$ of his, Kieran ate $\frac{1}{4}$ and Peter ate $\frac{3}{8}$.

a Who ate the most?

b Who ate the least?

explanation 2a explanation 2b

Write the answers to questions 6 to 8 as fractions in their lowest terms.

6 Write each fraction in its lowest terms.

a 28 as a fraction of 30

b 12 as a fraction of 15

c 20 as a fraction of 24

d 10 as a fraction of 6

e 180 as a fraction of 100

f 200 as a fraction of 150

g 360 as a fraction of 240

h 130 as a fraction of 75

7 a What fraction of 1 m is 50 cm?

b What fraction of 1 m is 35 mm?

c What fraction of 7 km is 2350 m?

d What fraction of 1 kg is 250 g?

e What fraction of 10 kg is 300 g?

f What fraction of 1 hour is 20 minutes?

| 1 km = 1000 m |
| 1 m = 100 cm |
| 1 m = 1000 mm |
| 1 kg = 1000 g |

8 Brenda is downloading a 120 MB file to her computer.

When 75 MB have been downloaded, what fraction of the file has been downloaded?

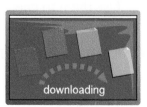

downloading

explanation 3a   explanation 3b   explanation 3c

9 Convert each percentage into a fraction in its lowest terms and then into a decimal.

a   50%   b   25%   c   20%   d   75%   e   65%

f   15%   g   45%   h   60%   i   90%   j   85%

10 Convert each percentage into a fraction in its lowest terms and then into a decimal.

a   28%   b   82%   c   52%   d   33%   e   18%

f   48%   g   72%   h   63%   i   175%   j   235%

11 Convert these decimals into percentages.

a   0.62   b   0.78   c   0.16   d   0.35   e   0.48

f   0.07   g   0.02   h   0.99   i   1.25   j   1.05

12 Convert these fractions into percentages.

Round your answers to one decimal place.

a $\dfrac{2}{10}$ b $\dfrac{2}{5}$ c $\dfrac{3}{4}$ d $\dfrac{16}{20}$ e $\dfrac{19}{25}$

f $\dfrac{19}{50}$ g $\dfrac{11}{15}$ h $\dfrac{11}{12}$ i $\dfrac{28}{35}$ j $\dfrac{1}{8}$

13 Copy and complete this table.

Percentage	Fraction	Decimal
	$\dfrac{9}{12}$	
		0.37
15%		
	$\dfrac{3}{8}$	
		0.445

14 In a 100-year period, a water molecule spends 98 years in the ocean, 20 months as ice, $\frac{1}{2}$ a month in lakes and rivers and less than $\frac{1}{4}$ of a month in the atmosphere.

What percentage of its time does a water molecule spend in these forms?

   a in the ocean   b as ice

(explanation 4a) (explanation 4b)

15 Use known facts to find these amounts.

   a 10% of 120   b 25% of 240   c 15% of 200

   d 45% of 360   e 75% of 96   f 80% of 60

16 Find these amounts. Round your answers to two decimal places.

   a 37% of 200   b 18% of 140   c 89% of 450

   d 34% of £80   e 18% of 96 cm   f 63% of 586 g

   g 62% of £134   h 79% of €270   i 12% of 168 km

You will need to use a calculator for these.

17 A dog weighs 40 kg. 60% of its total mass is water.

What is the mass of this water?

18 Brigit surveyed all 620 pupils in her school.

Some of her survey results are in this table.

Wear glasses	Have a dog	Did homework last night	Play a sport at school
15%	45%	85%	30%

How many pupils

   a wear glasses?   b have a dog?

   c did homework last night?   d play a sport at school?

19 42% of people have blood type O and 44% have blood type A.

    a Out of 850 patients in St Mary's Hospital, how many of each blood type would you expect to have?

    b In a class of 26 pupils, how many of blood type O would you expect to have? Round your answer sensibly.

---

explanation 5

20 Work these out.

    a 16 as a percentage of 20   **b** 12 as a percentage of 48

    c 15 as a percentage of 75   **d** 120 as a percentage of 300

    e 32 as a percentage of 160   **f** 6 as a percentage of 120

    g 260 as a percentage of 650   **h** 145 as a percentage of 1015

    i 168 as a percentage of 224   **j** 375 as a percentage of 1000

21 Find these amounts.

    a 8 as a percentage of 20   **b** 35 as a percentage of 175

    c 45 as a percentage of 50   **d** £90 as a percentage of £200

    e £150 as a percentage of £500   **f** £77 as a percentage of £140

22 Ishant wanted to buy a new stereo that cost £350.

He had saved £140.

What percentage of the price had he saved?

---

explanation 6a   explanation 6b

23 Work these out.

    a Increase 70 by 10%   **b** Increase 360 by 30%   **c** Increase 140 by 15%

    d Increase 96 by 75%   **e** Increase 20 by 85%   **f** Increase 348 by 25%

Alex began part **a** like this:

> 10% of 70 = 0.10 × 70 = 7
>
> 70 + increase of 10% =

Copy and complete his working to find the answer.

24 Find the cost of these items after a 24% price rise.

   a An off-road bike costing £590   **b** A mobile phone costing £127

   c A digital camera costing £165   **d** A sport watch costing £78

25 Corinne makes bags for a local shop.
The materials for each bag cost her £15.

> Always round answers to money problems sensibly.

   a She adds 30% to the cost price when she sells them to the shop.

      How much does she get for each bag?

   b The shop makes 25% profit on the bags. What does the shop sell them for?

26 Work these out.

   a Decrease 12 by 50%   **b** Decrease 200 by 80%

   c Decrease 120 by 15%   **d** Decrease 48 by 75%

   e Decrease 800 by 4%   **f** Decrease 320 by 60%

27 Find the cost of these items after a 16% price reduction.

   a A Nintendo game costing £32   **b** A leather sofa costing £485

   c A microwave costing £87   **d** A laptop computer costing £380

28 Dress4Less had a sale with 40% off all clothing.

   a How much did Kayla pay for a dress that was originally £98?

   b After two weeks the prices dropped again giving a further 20% off the sale price.

      If she had waited, how much would the dress have cost Kayla then?

29 Pravin thought that an increase of 20% followed by a decrease of 20% is greater than an increase of 10% followed by a decrease of 10%. Is he correct?

> Hint: What answers would you get if you had £100?

(explanation 7)

30 To find the percentage increase from 48 to 60, Luke started like this.

Actual increase = 60 – 48 = ☐

$\dfrac{\text{Actual increase}}{\text{Original amount}} = \dfrac{☐}{60}$

Percentage increase = $\dfrac{☐ \times ☐}{60}$% = ☐%

Copy and complete his working.

31 Find these percentage increases or decreases.

a   An increase from 40 to 50

b   An increase from 25 to 30

c   A decrease from 60 to 45

d   A decrease from 96 to 24

e   An increase from 150 to 250

f   A decrease from 320 to 280

32 A car depreciated in value from £5400 to £3600.

What percentage depreciation is this?

33 Three sports clubs could not agree on which club had had the biggest change in their membership.

Club	Membership 2000	Membership 2010
Chiefs	345	428
Red Devils	986	691
Rangers	589	835

Use the table to find which club had the biggest percentage change (increase or decrease).

Using ratios

- Understanding the relationship between fractions, percentages and ratios
- Simplifying ratios
- Dividing a quantity in a given ratio
- Solving problems using direct proportion

Keywords

You should know

explanation 1a   explanation 1b   explanation 1c

1 For each diagram find

   i   the ratio of the coloured part to the non-coloured part

   ii the proportion of the diagram that is coloured

a 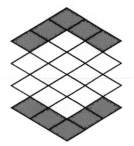   b 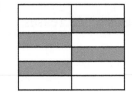   c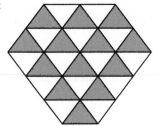

2 Write down the percentage of the diagram that is *not* coloured for each of the diagrams in question 1.

3 Copy each diagram. Shade each diagram so that the **shaded : unshaded** areas are in the given ratio.

   a   3:1   b   2:7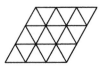

4 Write the proportion of the diagram that is shaded for each of the diagrams you drew in question 3 as a fraction in its lowest terms.

5 Write down the proportion of blue and red sticks in each of these ratios.

All ratios are in the form blue sticks : red sticks.

a $3:7$ b $12:19$ c $21:8$ d $13:7$ e $23:25$ f $32:33$

6 Mr Green planted his summer vegetable garden with the following:

6 tomato plants   8 lettuce plants

a row of 12 spring onions   3 cucumber plants

10 runner bean plants   3 courgette plants

a   Write the ratio of tomato plants to runner bean plants to courgette plants.

b   What proportion of his plants were lettuce plants?

c   Write the proportion of vegetables in his garden that were spring onions as a percentage.

| explanation 2a | explanation 2b |

7 Simplify these ratios.

a $4:12$ b $6:15$ c $24:18$ d $25:60$

e $45:72$ f $55:121$ g $50:125$ h $24:42$

i $63:51$ j $32:96$ k $40:12$ l $140:260$

m $225:500$ n $102:144$ o $2450:3000$ p $4500:750$

8 Find the missing digits that make these true.

a $5\square:96 = 7:\square2$

b $90:3\square0 = \square:33$

c $3\square:65 = 3:\square$

d $1\square2:\square6 = 11:\square$

9 Bella got these answers wrong in her maths test. What mistakes did she make?
Find the correct answers.

    a £1:45p = 1:45   **b** 5 minutes:1 hour = 5:1

    c 1 km:100 m = 1000:1   **d** 20p:£4 = 5:1

10 Write each ratio in its simplest form.

    a £2:40p   **b** 250 g:1 kg   **c** 126 cm:3 m

    d 6 hours:3 days   **e** 75 cm:6 m   **f** 4 km:800 m

    g 36 minutes:1 day   **h** 6 litres:360 ml   **i** 45 seconds:3 hours

> **explanation 3**

11 The pie chart shows the results of a
survey of 40 pupils on the time spent
doing homework per night.

    a What proportion of pupils do
exactly one hour of homework?

    b What is the ratio of pupils doing
45 minutes to those doing one hour?

    c What is the ratio of pupils doing
less than one hour to those doing
more than one hour?

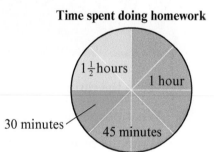

Time spent doing homework

12 This 4 m length of rope was cut into five sections for parts to make a rope ladder.

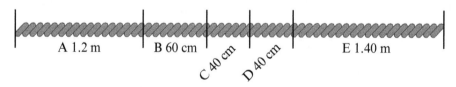

    A 1.2 m   B 60 cm   C 40 cm   D 40 cm   E 1.4 m

    a What is the ratio of the lengths of section A to section B?

    b What percentage of the rope is cut into sections less than 45 cm long?

    c What is the ratio of the lengths of sections C to D?
Give the ratio in its simplest form.

13 Divide each amount in the given ratio.

    a 24 in the ratio $2:4$ **b** 63 in the ratio $4:5$ **c** 64 in the ratio $3:5$

    d 90 in the ratio $3:7$ **e** 55 in the ratio $5:6$ **f** 75 in the ratio $2:3$

    g 132 in the ratio $5:7$ **h** 500 in the ratio $1:4$ **i** 120 in the ratio $2:3$

14 Jeetan spent £140 on clothes and cinema tickets in the ratio $5:2$.

How much money did he spend on each?

*15 The local amusement park sells family tickets, adult tickets and child tickets.

The ratio of numbers of tickets sold, family : adult : child, is $4:2:5$.

During the school holiday they sold 1320 tickets.

    a How many family tickets did they sell?

    b How many *more* child tickets did they sell than adult tickets?

explanation 4

16 Write these ratios in the form $1:m$.
Round to one decimal place (1 d.p.) if necessary.

    a $10:32$ **b** $4:15$ **c** $3:8$ **d** $8:21$ **e** $36:80$

17 Write these ratios in the form $m:1$.
Round to 1 d.p. if necessary.

    a $33:4$ **b** $69:23$ **c** $11:3$ **d** $42:8$ **e** $47:13$

18 The ratio of tries scored to tries converted for the Lowlanders rugby team is $18:5$ and for the Clansmen it is $15:4$.

Which team has the better conversion rate?

19 Which of these two dresses has the greater proportion of Lycra to other fibres?

Show your working.

Lycra : other fibres
3 : 7

Lycra : other fibres
4 : 9

explanation 5

20 This table shows the quantities of red and yellow paint needed to make orange paint.

Red paint (litres)	3	6	9	ii	36	iv
Yellow paint (litres)	5	10	i	35	iii	100

a   What is the ratio of red paint to yellow paint?

b   Find the missing amounts **i**, **ii**, **iii** and **iv**.

21 Michael drew a scale drawing of a model boat. He used a scale of 6:25.

The height of the mast of the model boat is 525 mm.

How long should the mast be on his drawing?

22 Jamie wants to use this recipe to feed 12 people.

a   Adapt the quantities for 12 people.

b   Jamie discovers that she has 375 g of butter and decides to use it all and adapt the recipe to match.

How many people will this be enough for?

Apple pie (for 4)

3 large apples
25 g brown sugar
200 g flour
75 g butter (or margarine)
50 g castor sugar
1 tablespoon water to mix

23 The ratio of the dimensions of the photograph shown are 9:4.

a   Find the length, *l*, of the picture.

b   Another photograph has dimensions in the ratio 11:5.

The shorter side is 15 cm.

What is the length of the other side?

Mental methods

- Using mental strategies to solve problems involving integers
- Using mental strategies to solve problems using fractions, decimals and percentages
- Using powers and roots
- Estimating to check solutions to problems

Keywords

You should know

explanation 1a　explanation 1b

Do not use a calculator for these questions.

1　a　$16 + 4 \times 3 - 7$　　b　$8 + 24 \div 6$　　　c　$25 - 4 \times 2$

　　d　$7 + 8 \times 3 - 4$　　e　$45 - 30 \div 5$　　　f　$30 \div 2 + 5 \times 4$

　　g　$19 - 32 \div 4 + 7$　　h　$12 + 6 \div 3 \times 2$

2　a　$(5 + 6) \times 4$　　b　$(15 - 8) \times (4 + 5)$　　c　$(34 - 6) \div 7$

　　d　$2(15 - 9)$　　　e　$(15 - 7) \div (3 + 1)$　　f　$5(23 + 9 - 2)$

　　g　$56 \div (6 + 2)$　　h　$(35 - 5) \div (4 + 2)$

3　a　$20 - 3^2$　　b　$(3 + 4)^2$　　c　$5^2 + 8$　　　d　2×4^2

　　e　$25 + 2^2 - 20$　　f　$(12 - 7)^2$　　g　$(8 - 2 \times 3)^2$　　h　$35 + (2 + 6)^2$

4　Copy these statements and add brackets to make them correct.

　　a　$3 + 5 \times 2 = 16$　　b　$4 \times 8 - 5 = 12$　　　c　$2 \times 9 + 7 = 32$

　　d　$4 + 8 \div 2 = 6$　　　e　$3 \times 20 - 12 = 24$　　f　$6 + 5 \times 5 - 2 = 33$

5　Find the answers to these.

　　a　$\dfrac{28}{3 + 4}$　　b　$\dfrac{36 \div 2}{9}$　　c　$\dfrac{12 + 15}{11 - 2}$　　d　$\dfrac{8 \times 2}{5 - 1}$　　e　$\dfrac{15 \times 2 - 5}{10 \div 2}$

　　f　$\dfrac{(1 + 2 \times 4)^2}{2 + 1}$　　g　$\dfrac{5 \times 62}{5 \times 2}$　　h　$\dfrac{5 - 2^2}{(2 + 1)^2}$　　i　$\dfrac{8^2 + 6}{7^2 + 1}$　　j　$\dfrac{(45 \div 5)^2}{4 \times 2 + 1}$

149

6 Jackson read out a calculation from his maths textbook. He said:

'6 plus 2 multiplied by 3 squared minus 4 equals 38'

His brother said this didn't make sense.

Write down the calculation and add brackets to make it true.

(explanation 2a)   (explanation 2b)   (explanation 2c)

7 Find the answers to these.

a	$-4 + 8$	b	$2 - -3$	c	$5 + -1$	d	$-4 - -3$

a $-4 + 8$ b $2 - -3$ c $5 + -1$ d $-4 - -3$

e $-7 + -3$ f $5 - -2$ g $6 + -4$ h $-4 + -5$

> You could think about moving up and down a number line to help.

8 A large shopping complex has 4 parking levels below ground and 11 levels of shops and offices above ground.

The floor levels on the lift are labelled as shown in this diagram.

What level do these people end up on?

a Cherie is on basement level −3 and goes up 5 levels.

b Curtis is on level 8 and goes down 12 levels

c Lee is on basement level −1 and goes up 9 levels.

d Princeton is on level 2 and goes down 5 levels.

e Sam starts at ground level 0, goes up 9 levels and then down 12 levels.

> level 10
> level 9
> level 8
> level 7
> level 6
> level 5
> level 4
> level 3
> level 2
> level 1
> ground level 0
> basement level −1
> basement level −2
> basement level −3
> basement level −4

9 The temperature in Mooseville, Canada, ranges from −25°C to 15°C.

Find the new temperature after each rise or fall in the temperature.

	Starting temperature	Temperature rise or fall	New temperature
a	−20°C	rise of 17°C	
b	7°C	fall of 16°C	
c	−12°C	rise of 18°C	
d	11°C	fall of 17°C	
e	−3°C	rise of 14°C	

10 Find the answers to these.

a $-12 + -23$

b $34 - -21$

c $45 + -19$

d $-31 - -32$

e $-51 + -23 - 18$

f $75 + -34 - -12$

11 Work out these multiplications.

a 5×-6

b -4×-7

c -8×20

d -30×-6

e 12×-10

f -90×-2

g -40×8

h 15×-5

12 Work out these divisions.

a $-8 \div 4$

b $28 \div -7$

c $-72 \div -9$

d $45 \div -9$

e $-64 \div -8$

f $36 \div -4$

g $125 \div -25$

h $120 \div -4$

13 On Friday Winston had £234 in his current account at the bank.

a At the weekend he went shopping and spent £309.

How much was his current account overdrawn now?

b On Monday he deposited £268 from his savings into his current account.

How much was in his current account now?

14 One Friday night in Mooseville, Canada, the temperature was $-7°C$.

On Sunday night it was 9°C colder.

What was the temperature?

explanation 3a | explanation 3b | explanation 3c | explanation 3d

15 Find answers to these mentally.

a $460 + 125 + 340 + 375 + 130$

b $67 + 242 + 333 + 58$

c $5.7 + 8.1 + 6.3$

d $16.48 + 5.52$

e 34×50

f 16×25

g $650 \div 25$

h 60×80

i 150×30

j $640 \div 8$

k 3.8×25

l $\frac{1}{4} \times 124$

m 25% of 48

n 0.75×64

16 Bags of potatoes at the supermarket weigh 2.8 kg each.
How much will 25 bags weigh?

17 Shona cut a ribbon into four lengths of 65 cm, 1.24 m, 2.35 m and 76 cm.
How long was the ribbon before it was cut up?

18 Musta had £340 to go shopping. A new football strip cost 25% of his money.
How much did it cost?

19 The probability that Bradley will beat Zac at the gaming competition is 0.6.
Out of 35 games how many would you expect Bradley to win?

Expected number of wins	=	number of games played	×	probability of winning

20 Use multiplication and division and place value to answer these.

a   3000 × 500   b   2400 ÷ 60   c   2700 × 300   d   4200 ÷ 700

e   54 000 ÷ 6000   f   720 × 3000   g   2.4 × 200   h   600 × 0.8

i   3.2 × 3000   j   2.4 ÷ 100   k   3.6 ÷ 200   l   670 000 × 300

21 A shelf in the school library holds 70 books.

Approximately how many shelves of the same size will be needed to hold 6300 books?

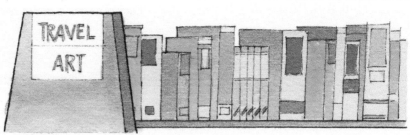

22 Find the answers to these using mental strategies.

a   6.7 + 4.81 + 2.3   b   19.6 + 8.92 − 3.6   c   12.75 − 2.8 + 2.25

d   9.96 + 8.04 − 12   e   11.34 − 5.9 + 2.36   f   32.68 + 2.99

g   86.47 + 3.98   h   46.23 − 4.99   i   17.41 − 6.98

j $\frac{3}{4} + \frac{5}{8} + \frac{1}{4}$ k $\frac{2}{3} + 1\frac{1}{3} + \frac{3}{5}$ l $2\frac{1}{2} + 3\frac{5}{8} + 1\frac{1}{2}$

23 Use mental strategies to solve these.

a 16×32	b 45×14	c 125×32	d $64 \div 16$
e 56.8×25	f $764 \div 4$	g $24.8 \div 4$	h 20.6×23
i 3.7×60	j 53×11	k 29×34	l $648 \div 27$
m 36×15	n $240 \div 16$	o 6.4×50	p 18×42
q 1.56×70	r $860 \div 4$		

24 Jenni made a fruit punch with this recipe.

How many litres of punch will this make?

$1 \text{ litre} = 1000 \text{ ml}$

Fruit Punch

3.85 litres lemonade

780 ml lemon concentrate

550 ml orange concentrate

1.4 litres ginger ale

25 On average Kev's football team scored 2.8 goals per game last season.

They played 25 games.

How many goals did Kev's team score in total?

explanation 4a   explanation 4b   explanation 4c

26 Simplify these expressions.

a $4 \times 4 \times 4 \times 4$

b $5 \times 5 \times 5 \times 5 \times 5 \times 5$

c $6 \times 6 \times 7 \times 7 \times 7$

d $6 \times 6 \times 6 \times 6 \times 8 \times 8 \times 8$

e $3 \times 3 \times 3 \times 5 \times 5 \times 7 \times 7$

f $9 \times 10 \times 10 \times 15 \times 15 \times 15$

27 a Copy this table. Fill in the empty white cells.

x	2	3	4	5	6	7	8	9	10
x^2	4								
$\sqrt{x}$									

b The green cells do not have whole-number square roots.

   i Is $\sqrt{5}$ closer to 2 or to 3?   ii Is $\sqrt{8}$ closer to 2 or to 3?

28 Find these square roots.

    a $\sqrt{16}$ b $\sqrt{64}$ c $\sqrt{36}$ d $\sqrt{100}$ e $\sqrt{25}$ f $\sqrt{81}$ g $\sqrt{49}$

29 Steph thinks that $\sqrt{19} \approx 4$ because 19 is closer to 16 than 25.

    Find approximate values for these square roots.

    a $\sqrt{96}$ b $\sqrt{38}$ c $\sqrt{69}$

    d $\sqrt{22}$ e $\sqrt{90}$ f $\sqrt{51}$

> $\approx$ means 'is approximately equal to'.

30 Work these out.

    a 3^3 b 5^3 c 10^3 d $\sqrt[3]{8}$ e $\sqrt[3]{64}$

31 a Work out the area of this square.   b Find the side, s, of this square.

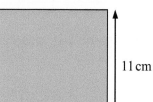

11 cm

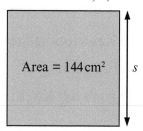

Area = 144 cm² s

    c Work out the volume of this cube.   d Find the side length, l, of the cube.

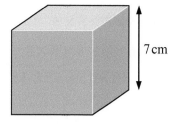

7 cm

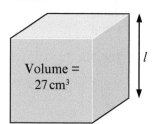

Volume = 27 cm³ l

> explanation 5a   explanation 5b   explanation 5c

32 Abbie's cake recipe uses 250 g of flour for one cake. She baked six cakes for a party.

    Each of Abbie's friends worked out a different total for the amount of flour Abbie used.

    Jacinta 5 kg   Lucy 75 g   Joelle 1.25 kg   Missie 500 g

    Which answer is most sensible?

33 Check these answers using inverse operations. Which ones are wrong?

a $23 \times 5 = 120$ b $87 \div 3 = 29$ c $326 - 194 = 134$ d $6 \times 52 = 312$

34 a   Which of these is equivalent to 24×36?

   A $12 \times 2 \times 12 \times 3$ B 48×18 C $48 \times 12 \times 2$ D $24 \times 6 \times 6$

   b   Find another equivalent calculation that could be used to check the answer.

35 Pick a possible correct answer to each calculation. Explain your choice.

a 79×15 A   1185   B   1423   C   1200

b 2×1.3 A   39.8   B   41.6   C   40.2

c 2.6×57 A   154.8   B   148.2   C   144.5

36 Estimate the answer to each calculation.

Do not find the exact answer.

a 4.5×3.8 b $7.8 \div 1.85$ c $128 \div 9.8$ d $96.4 \div 12$

e 8.4×7.8 f 346×12 g 5.8×9.4 h 111×89

i 38.7×9.2 j $523 \div 97$ k 489×224 l $317 \div 6.7$

37 Estimate the answer to each of these.

a   An ounce is about 28.35 g. How many ounces are there in 585 g?

b   A nautical mile is approximately 1.853 km. How many km are there in 223 nautical miles?

c   A litre is approximately 1.759 pints. How many pints are there in 84 litres?

38 On holiday Jo's family travelled 234.7 km on the first day. On the next four days they travelled 233.6 km, 87.3 km, 158.2 km and 217.4 km.

a   Estimate how far they travelled altogether.

b   Work out the total distance they travelled.

c   The car travels 18 km on 1 litre of petrol.

   Approximately how much petrol did they use?

Perimeter

- Finding the perimeter of different shapes
- Solving problems involving perimeter

Keywords

You should know

explanation 1

1 These shapes are drawn on a centimetre-square grid.
Find the perimeter of each shape.

a 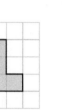   b   c

2 Find the perimeter of each of these shapes.

a
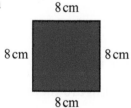
8 cm
8 cm   8 cm
8 cm

b
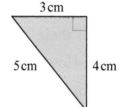
3 cm
5 cm   4 cm

c
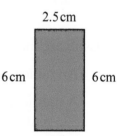
2.5 cm
6 cm   6 cm
2.5 cm

d
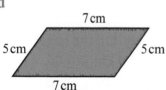
7 cm
5 cm   5 cm
7 cm

e
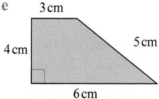
3 cm
4 cm   5 cm
6 cm

3 Look at the square in part **a** of question **2**. How can you find the perimeter of
this square without adding up the lengths of all the sides?

4 How can you find the perimeter of the rectangle or the parallelogram in parts **c**
and **d** of question **2** without adding up the lengths of all the sides?

explanation 2

5 Work out the perimeter of each shape without adding up all the side lengths.

Show your methods clearly.

a
12 mm

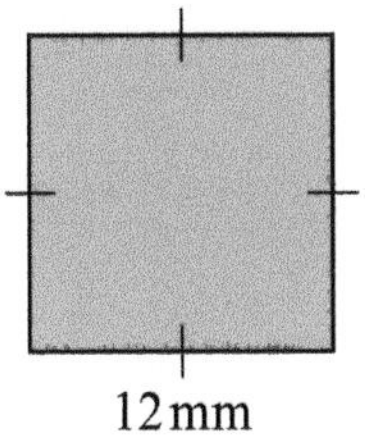

b
15 cm
8 cm

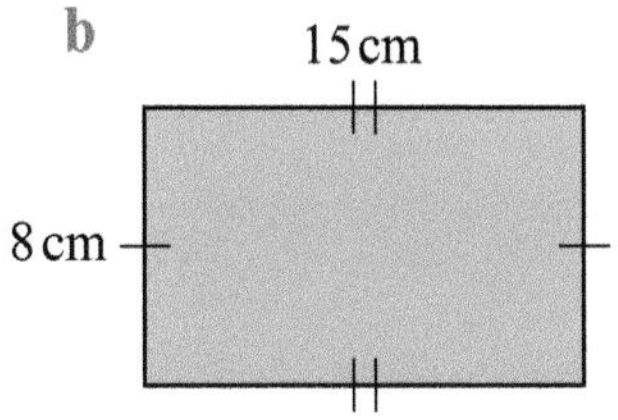

c
20 m

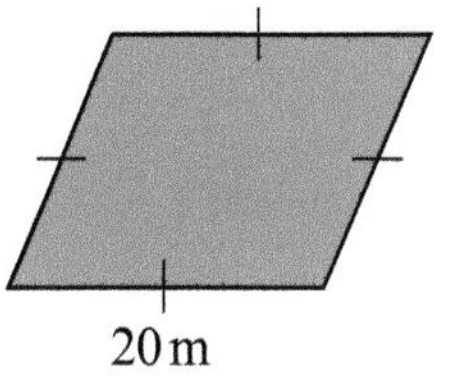

d
13 cm
27 cm

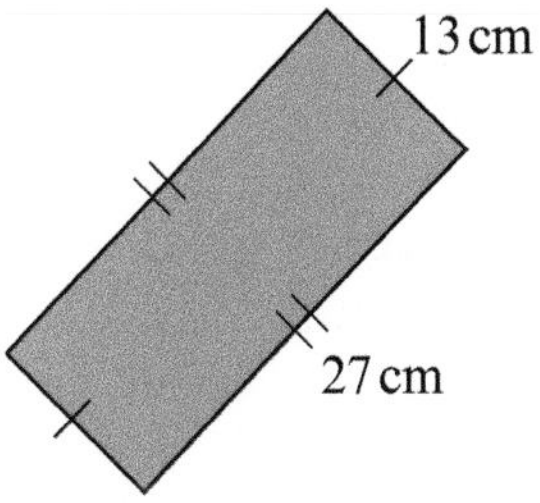

e
6 cm
8 cm

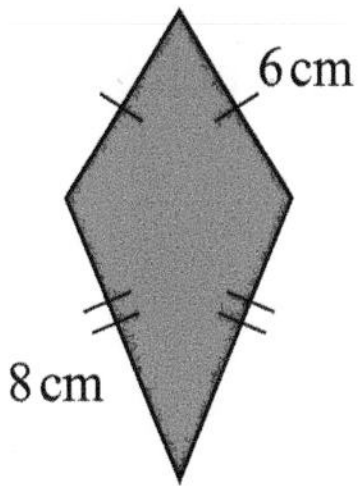

f
4 m

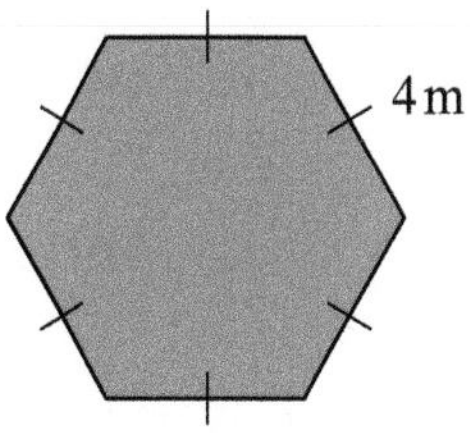

6 a A square has side length 15 cm. What is the perimeter of the square?

b The perimeter of a square is 100 cm. What is the length of each side?

7 a A rectangle has length 12 cm and width 8 cm. What is its perimeter?

b A rectangle has perimeter 60 m. Its length is 20 m. What is its width?

8 a An equilateral triangle has perimeter 21 cm.
What are the lengths of its sides?

b An isosceles triangle has two sides of length 12 cm each.
Its perimeter is 30 cm. What is the length of its third side?

9 This question is about a rhombus and a parallelogram.

a A rhombus has perimeter 36 cm. What is the length of its sides?

b A parallelogram has sides 6 cm and p cm. Its perimeter is 20 cm.
What is the length p cm?

10 a A regular pentagon has side length 10 cm. What is its perimeter?

b A regular polygon has side length 8 cm and has a perimeter of 64 cm.

   i How many sides does the polygon have?

   ii What is the name of this polygon?

explanation 3

11 Look at each shape.

   i Copy the shapes and add the missing side lengths of each shape.

   ii Find the perimeter of each shape.

a

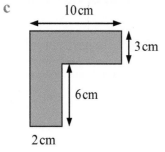

b

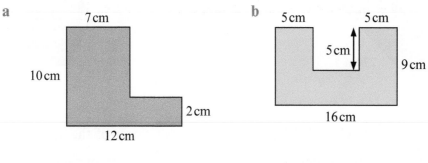

c

d

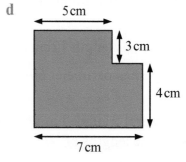

e

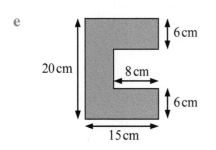

f

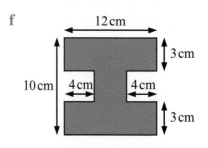

12 Look at each shape.

    i Find the lengths marked x and y on each shape.

    ii Find the perimeter of each shape.

a

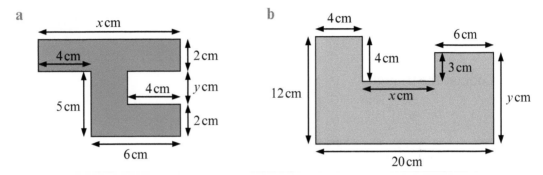

b

13 Shape A is an equilateral triangle and shape B is a square.

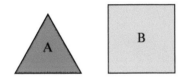

Daniel put the two shapes together to make a pentagon.

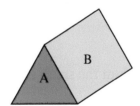

  a Danuta said: 'The perimeter of the pentagon is the same as the perimeters of shapes A and B added together.'

    Explain why Danuta is wrong.

  b The perimeter of the pentagon is 50 cm.

    What are the perimeters of triangle A and square B?

14 Peter was asked to find the perimeter of this right-angled triangle.

He said the perimeter was 12 cm.

Was Peter correct?

Explain how you know.

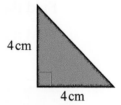

4 cm

4 cm

15 Look at the triangle.

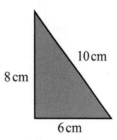

10 cm

8 cm

6 cm

Four of these triangles were put together to make a square within a square.

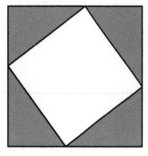

How much bigger is the perimeter of the large square than the small square?

16 Four triangles like the triangle in question **15** are put together to make these shapes.

Find the perimeter of each shape.

a   b   c

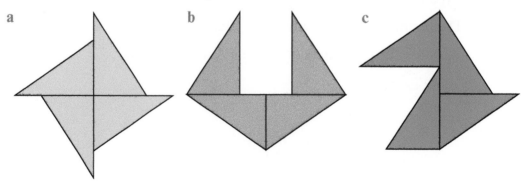

Area

- Calculating the area of compound shapes
- Calculating the area of a triangle
- Calculating the area of a parallelogram and trapezium
- Solving problems involving area

Keywords

You should know

explanation 1

1 The shapes are on a centimetre-square grid. Find the area of each shape.

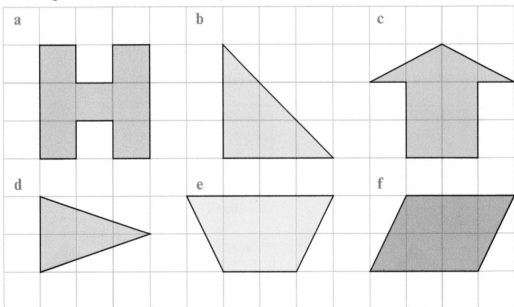

2 The shapes are on a centimetre-square grid. Estimate the area of each shape.

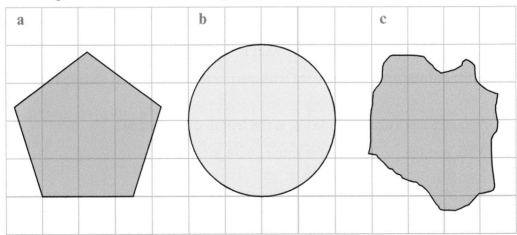

161

3 The diagram shows a rectangle with base 5 cm and height 4 cm.

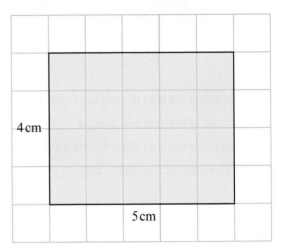

 a How can you use the base and the height to work out how many square centimetres are in the rectangle?

 b What is the area of the rectangle?

 c Peter said: 'The perimeter of the rectangle is 18 cm^2.'

  What mistake has Peter made?

> explanation 2

4 Work out the area and perimeter of each rectangle or square.

Don't forget to include the units in your answers.

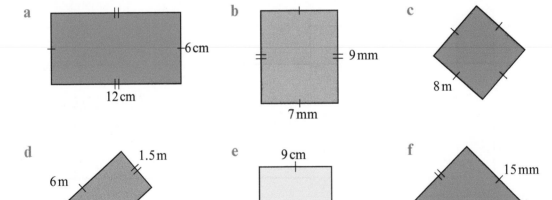

5 a A square has perimeter 80 cm. What is the length of each side?

 b Work out the area of a square with perimeter 80 cm.

6 a A square has area 49 m^2. What is the length of each side?

 b Work out the perimeter of a square with area 49 m^2.

7 **a** A rectangle has base 12 cm and area 36 cm². What is its height?

b Another rectangle also has area 36 cm². Its height is 4 cm. What is its base?

explanation 3

8 Copy and complete this area calculation.

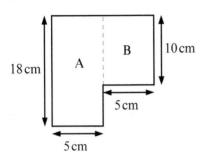

Area A = $\square$ × $\square$ = $\square$ cm²

Area B = $\square$ × $\square$ = $\square$ cm²

Total area $\quad$ = $\square$ cm²

9 Look at each shape.

   i Work out the missing lengths.

   ii Find the area of each shape.

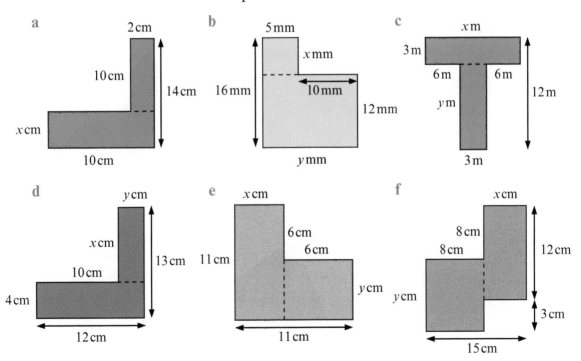

explanation 4a   explanation 4b

10 Look at the diagram.

   a Use the diagram to explain how you can find the area of the shaded triangle from the area of the rectangle.

   b What is the area of the shaded triangle?

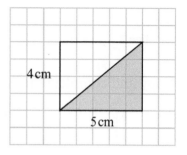

4 cm

5 cm

11 Calculate the area of each triangle.

   a

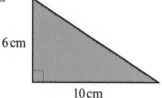

   6 cm

   10 cm

   b

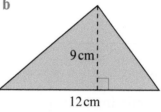

   9 cm

   12 cm

   c

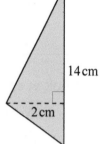

   14 cm

   2 cm

12 Which method below gives the area of the triangle?

Explain your answer.

   A $17 \times 24 \div 2 = 204 \, \text{cm}^2$

   B $17 \times 25 \div 2 = 212.5 \, \text{cm}^2$

   C $17 \times 26 \div 2 = 221 \, \text{cm}^2$

   D $25 \times 26 \div 2 = 325 \, \text{cm}^2$

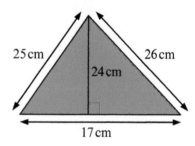

25 cm   26 cm

24 cm

17 cm

13 Calculate the area of each triangle.

   a

   10 cm

   6 cm

   12 cm

   b

   6 cm

   4 cm

   10 cm

   c

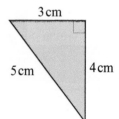

   3 cm

   5 cm   4 cm

14 Calculate the area of each triangle.

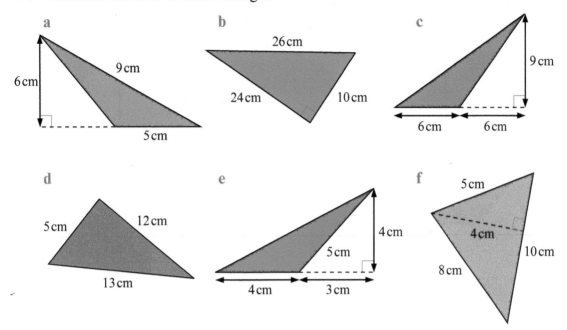

a

6 cm

9 cm

5 cm

b

26 cm

24 cm   10 cm

c

9 cm

6 cm   6 cm

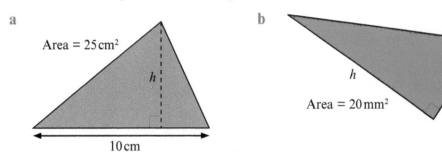

d

5 cm   12 cm

13 cm

e

4 cm

5 cm

4 cm   3 cm

f

5 cm

4 cm

8 cm   10 cm

15 The area and the base length of each triangle are given.

Calculate the height of each triangle.

a

Area = 25 cm²

h

10 cm

b

h

Area = 20 mm²

4 mm

explanation 5

16 Sarah says: 'The area of the parallelogram is the same as the area of a rectangle.'

a What are the length and the width of the rectangle that has the same area as this parallelogram?

b What is the area of this parallelogram?

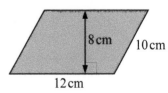

8 cm   10 cm

12 cm

17 Calculate the area of each parallelogram.

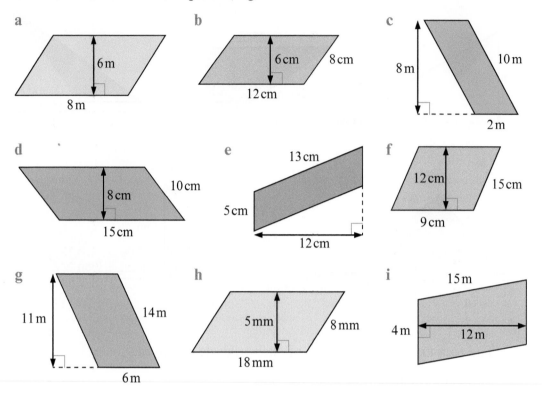

a

6 m
8 m

b

6 cm   8 cm
12 cm

c

8 m   10 m
2 m

d

8 cm   10 cm
15 cm

e

13 cm
5 cm
12 cm

f

12 cm   15 cm
9 cm

g

11 m   14 m
6 m

h

5 mm   8 mm
18 mm

i

15 m
4 m   12 m

18 Work out the area of each shape

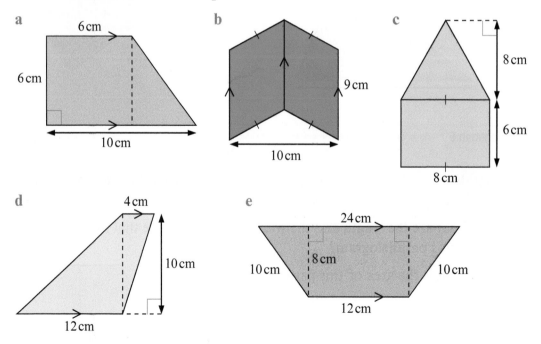

a

6 cm
6 cm
10 cm

b

9 cm
10 cm

c

8 cm
6 cm
8 cm

d

4 cm
10 cm
12 cm

e

24 cm
10 cm   8 cm   10 cm
12 cm

explanation 6

19 Look at the diagram.

a What is the area of the rectangle?

b What is the area of the triangle?

c Explain why the area of the blue part is $117\,m^2$.

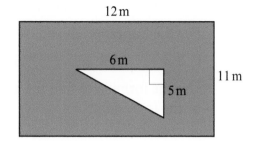

20 Work out the area of the coloured part of each diagram.

a

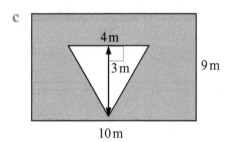

b

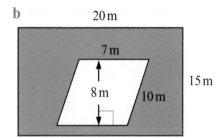

c

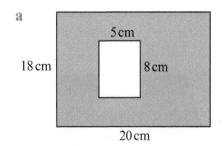

d

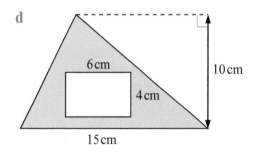

e

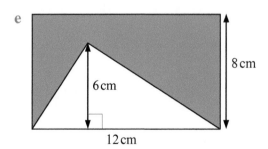

f

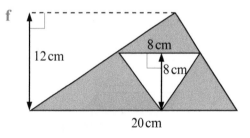

explanation 7a   explanation 7b

21 The formula for the area of a trapezium is $A = \frac{1}{2}(a + b)h$.

  a For the trapezium shown, what is the value of each of these?

   i h **ii** a **iii** b

  b Use the formula to find the area of the trapezium.

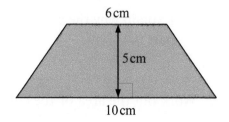

22 Calculate the area of each trapezium.

a

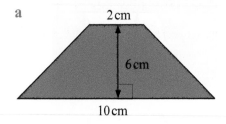

b

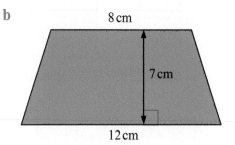

c

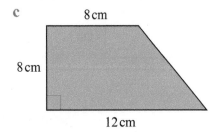

d

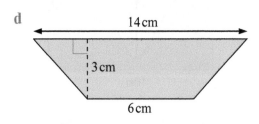

e

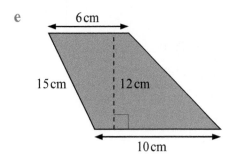

f

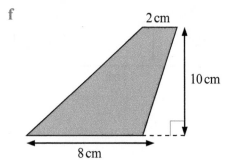

Statistical investigations

● Planning a statistical investigation to solve a problem

● Collecting data

Keywords

You should know

explanation 1

1 Some pupils in a class are going to investigate different problems.

What data will each need to collect?

a Jenny wants to compare the heights of boys and the heights of girls.

b Anil wants to investigate whether teachers or pupils are better at mental arithmetic.

c Pat wants to investigate the relationship between the size of a country's population and the area of the country.

d Sam wants to compare the weather in New York with the weather in London.

e Morgan wants to investigate what happens to the value of cars as they get older.

f Ahmed wants to investigate the relationship between the time pupils spend watching television and their exam results.

g Geoff wants to investigate whether boys or girls are better at maths.

h James wants to investigate the amount of time boys and girls spend playing sport outside school.

explanation 2a explanation 2b

2 Data is going to be collected to carry out some more investigations.

Copy and complete the table.

The first row has been completed for you.

	Investigation	Data will be collected from	Type of data (primary or secondary)
a	Taller people are heavier than shorter people.	Pupils in the school	Primary
b	It is hotter in Egypt than in Crete.		
c	The taller you are, the quicker your reaction time.		
d	The average length of television programmes is 30 minutes.		
e	Pupils who watch more television spend more time on the internet.		
f	The closer a pupil lives to school, the more homework they do.		
g	Girls read more books than boys.		

3 Tina wants to find out if it rains more in Newcastle or in Penzance.

a What data will she need for this investigation?

b Where could she get her data from?

4 Sumire wants to find out if taller children have longer arms than shorter children.

    a   What data will she need for this investigation?

    b   Where could she get her data from?

    c   How could she collect her data?

5 Richard wants to find out if football teams with more foreign players win more matches.

    a   What data will he need to collect for this investigation?

    b   Where could he get his data from?

> explanation 3a   explanation 3b

6 Design data collection sheets for these surveys or experiments.

    a   The number scored when a four-sided spinner is spun.

    b   Colours of cars in the school car park.

    c   The favourite sport of pupils in your year.

    d   The number of school books in school bags.

    e   The total scored when two dice are rolled together.

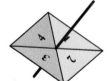

7 Design data collection sheets to collect these data.

    a   The number of words in the sentences of a book.

    b   The number of people at the cinema each afternoon one month.

    c   The shoe sizes of pupils in your maths class.

    d   The number of vehicles in the school car park at different times of the day.

    e   The number of pages in a selection of books.

explanation 4

8 Sam designs a questionnaire.

He gives it to his friends to fill in.

Some of his friends cannot fill in the questionnaire.

  a Explain why each of Sam's friends can't fill in the questionnaire.

  b Rewrite the questionnaire so that everyone can fill it in.

Sam's questionnaire

1 What type of mobile phone do you own?

Nokia ☐   Samsung ☐

2 How would you rate your mobile phone?

Average ☐   Good ☐   Excellent ☐

3 How much do you spend each week using your mobile phone?

0 – £2 ☐   £2 – £4 ☐   £4 – £6 ☐   £6 or more ☐

4 How many text messages do you send?

0 – 10 ☐   11 – 20 ☐   21 – 30 ☐   31 – 40 ☐

'I don't like my mobile phone; it's awful!'

'My mobile phone is a Motorola'

'I spend exactly £4 a week'

'I send 20 texts a day'

'I send 20 texts a month'

i   ii   iii   iv   v

9 Harry wants to find out how people use the local library.

He is interested in the number of times that people visit the library and how many books they borrow.

Write two questions that Harry could use in a questionnaire.

Each question should have some response boxes.

10 Jemilla wants to find out what her friends think about school dinners.

She wants to know how often her friends use the canteen, how much they spend and what their favourite meal is.

Write three questions that Jemilla could use.

Each question should include some response boxes.

11 Meg wants to find out how people use the local sports centre.

She wants to investigate what sports people play, what they think of the local sports centre, how often they use it and how far away from the sports centre they live.

Each question should include some response boxes.

12 Choose one of the following questions and plan your own investigation.

    i Write a statement to test.

    ii Explain how you will collect your data and how much data you will collect.

    iii Design a questionnaire or data collection sheet.

  a Do children who watch more television do less homework?

  b Do people who run faster have longer legs?

  c Are children quicker at writing text messages than adults?

  d Do 16-year-olds get more homework than 12-year-olds?

Interpreting and communicating

- Interpreting more complex graphs and diagrams
- Deciding which type of graph to draw

Keywords

You should know

explanation 1a   explanation 1b   explanation 1c

1 The bar chart shows the mean number of hours of sunshine per day each month in Madrid.

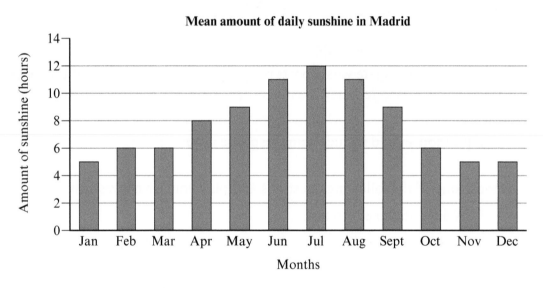

Mean amount of daily sunshine in Madrid

a Which month has the highest mean number of hours of sunshine per day?

b Which three months all have a mean of 6 hours of sunshine per day?

c Fred says: 'Most months have an average of more than 7 hours of sunshine per day'.

Is Fred correct? Give an explanation for your answer.

2 Greta surveys some houses in a street. She notes the type of house and whether or not it has a satellite dish. She displays her results in a two-way table.

	Terrace	Semi-detached	Detached	Total
Satellite dish	29	19	7	55
No satellite dish	8	15	2	25
Total	37	34	9	80

   a How many semi-detached houses have a satellite dish?

   b How many detached houses do not have a satellite dish?

   c Greta thinks that more houses in the street do not have a satellite dish than have one. Is she correct?
Give an explanation for your answer.

3 The pie chart shows the way all the pupils in a school travel to school.

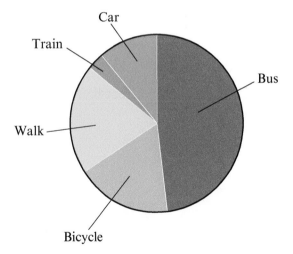

   a How do most pupils travel to school?

   b What is the least popular method of travelling to school?

   c Sahil says: 'More pupils travel to school by car than by bicycle.'
Is Sahil correct?
Give an explanation for your answer.

4 The dual bar chart shows the number of medals won by Great Britain and Australia in the 2008 Olympic games.

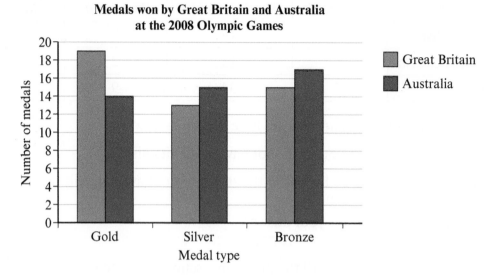

Medals won by Great Britain and Australia at the 2008 Olympic Games

a How many silver medals did Great Britain win?

b How many gold medals did Australia win?

c Which country won more bronze medals?

d Tony says: 'Australia won more medals in total then Great Britain.' Is Tony correct? Give a reason for your answer.

e Maria draws two pie chart to display the data.

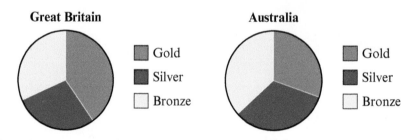

Does the bar chart or pie charts show the results more clearly? Explain your answer.

5 Dinesh asked his friends where they went on holiday last year.

The pie chart shows the results of his survey.

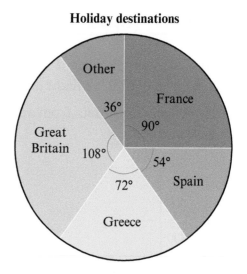

Holiday destinations

a   What fraction of the people surveyed went to France?

b   Which country was most frequently chosen for holidays?

c   Dinesh says: 'More people went to Spain than France.' Is Dinesh correct? Give a reason for your answer.

d   30 people went to France for their holiday. How many people took part in the survey?

6 The pie charts show the favourite subjects of some boys and some girls.

a   Which subject did most girls prefer?

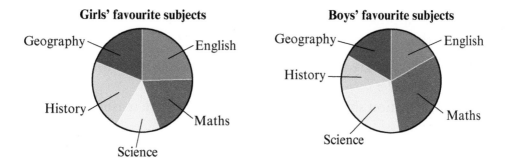

b   Which subject did most boys prefer?

c   Helen says that science was the least favourite subject for the boys and the girls. Is she correct? Give an explanation for your answer.

explanation 2a   explanation 2b

7   Alan wants to find out if there is a relationship between the distance travelled during an aeroplane flight and the cost of the flight.

He collects some data from an airline's website then uses the data to plot a scatter graph.

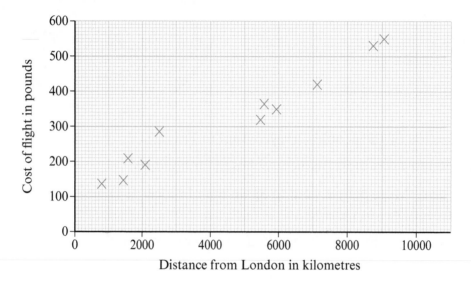

Distance from London in kilometres

a   How many of the flights were shorter than 5000 kilometres?

b   How many flights cost more than £400?

c   One of the points represents a flight from London to Miami.
    Miami is approximately 7100 km from London.
    Approximately how much did this flight cost?

d   Alan says: 'The greater the distance travelled, the more the flights cost.' Is Alan correct?
    Use information shown in the scatter graph to give reasons for your answer.

8 Paul lives in York. He thinks that the more it rains, the lower the temperature is. To test his idea, Paul collects some data about the weather in York.
He uses the data to draw this scatter graph.

Is Paul correct? Explain how you use the information shown in the graph to reach your conclusion.

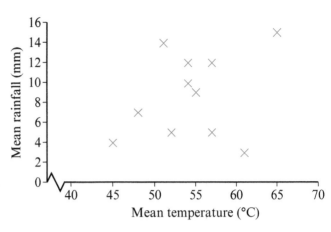

9 Anya is doing a geography project. Anya says: 'The higher the birth rate of a county, the lower the life expectancy in that country.' She collects some data from the internet.
She uses the data to draw a scatter graph.

Is Anya correct? Explain how you use the information shown in the graph to reach your conclusion.

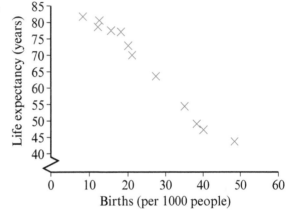

10 The ages of some Ford Fiestas and their values are shown in the scatter graph

What does the graph show about the relationship between the value of a Ford Fiesta and its age?

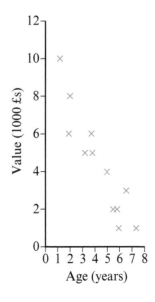

Written methods

- Using written methods for addition, subtraction, multiplication and division of decimals with differing numbers of decimal places
- Using problem solving skills with calculations involving money

Keywords

You should know

explanation 1

Do not use calculators for this topic.

1 Work out these additions.

a 23.6 + 11.7

b 42.7 + 25.9

c 54.7 + 49.5

d 19.43 + 24.05

e 7.54 + 25.52

f 72.59 + 8.67

g 1.874 + 34.503

h 24.798 + 37.607

i 4.56 + 81.48 + 37.42

j 11.37 + 35.82 + 8.77

k 234.534 + 4.603 + 21.062

2 Work these out.

a 51.05 + 45.921

b 2.806 + 96.3

c 34.8 + 23.74

d 45.5 + 124.64

e 420.53 + 916.9

f 793.354 + 53.04

g 2.99 + 48.031

h 54.72 + 179.098

i 36.84 + 372.7 + 111.98

j 45.8 + 813 + 67.52

k 648.805 + 43.7 + 0.337

l 3.462 + 73.072 + 104.006

3 Find the perimeter of each of these shapes.

a
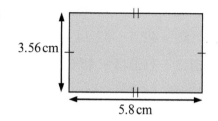
3.56 cm

5.8 cm

b
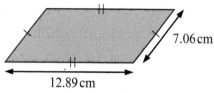
7.06 cm

12.89 cm

c
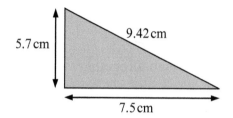
5.7 cm

9.42 cm

7.5 cm

d
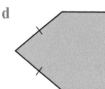

4.5 cm

6.78 cm

(explanation 2a)   (explanation 2b)

4 Work out these subtractions.

a 23.9 − 12.7   b 35.5 − 24.8   c 2.54 − 1.39

d 35.73 − 32.56   e 404.82 − 58.79   f 80.63 − 45.74

g 406.3 − 6.74   h 27.465 − 18.5   i 403.6 − 39.58

j 30.08 − 24.65   k 407.562 − 320.798   l 1073.4 − 891.5

5 Work these out.

a 57.9 − 30.4 − 5.2   b 37.05 − 11.13 − 8.7

c 24.7 − 9.1 − 5.6   d 13.6 − 4.71 − 3.4

e 40.3 − 7 − 21.7   f 31.83 − 6.4 − 23.54

g 102.43 − 64.7 − 11.38   h 64.2 − 6.74 − 46.3

i 211.453 − 45.84 − 20.303

6 Bob collected £115.23 selling items at a car boot sale.

Petrol to travel to the sale cost him £11.58.

He paid £14.95 for lunch.

How much of his sales money did he have left
after buying petrol and lunch?

7 Work out these mixed addition and subtraction calculations.

a $5.7 - 2.9 + 3.6$

b $8.04 + 22.7 - 15.46$

c $18.6 - 13.25 + 5.24$

d $4.56 - 43.5 + 62.34$

e $5.7 - 30.2 + 58.92 + 5$

f $61.3 - 11.043 + 45.617$

g $40.7 + 3.7 - 36.82 + 6.02$

h $12.45 - 6.2 + 5.6 + 24.031$

i $5.7 - 7.8 + 13.03 - 2.55$

8 Three sacks weigh 6.64 kg, 5.67 kg and 7.82 kg.

How much more or less than 20 kg do they weigh altogether?

9 At the school sports day James jumped 4.57 m in the long jump and 11.39 m in the triple jump.

The winner of the two events jumped a total of 17.08 m.

How many metres short of the winning total were James' jumps?

10 On three days of their holiday Desiree's family travelled 212.6 km, 144.65 km and 98.04 km.

a   How far did they travel in total?

b   Desiree estimated that they had travelled 450 km.

How much more or less than her estimate had they travelled?

11 Mohammed made 2.75 litres of orange squash.

He poured 0.68 litres and 0.89 litres into two flasks to take to soccer practice and drank a 0.35 litre glass of squash before he left home.

How much orange squash was left in the jug?

explanation 3a   explanation 3b   explanation 3c

12 Work out these multiplications.

    a 135×72 b 73×327 c 567×46 d 624×59 e 93×276

13 Work these out.

    a 8×45.6 b 36.8×15 c 34.2×12 d 6.8×32

    e 11.7×18 f 21×3.4 g 16.7×26 h 43×32.1

    i 61.4×31 j 19.8×36 k 24×35.8 l 53×18.6

    m 73×24.3 n 60.4×24 o 39.3×58

14 An antibiotic for dog flu is given every 24 hours.

The dosage is based on the body mass of the dog.

How much will be given to dogs with these weights?

    a   5 kg   b   18 kg   c   32 kg

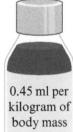

0.45 ml per kilogram of body mass

15 A restaurant buys fruit and vegetables from the market.
How much will the bill be for each of these?

    a   5.3 kg of apples at £1.20 a kg   b   3.6 kg of beans at £5.70 a kg

    c   5.1 kg of cherries at £8.70 a kg   d   7.9 kg of tomatoes at £4.70 a kg

    e   13.4 kg of potatoes at £1.90 a kg   f   4.8 kg of mushrooms at £14.10 a kg

16 The prices for petrol at the local petrol station are in the table.

    a   How much will it cost Peter to put 3.4 litres of unleaded petrol into his motorbike?

Unleaded petrol	£1.08 per litre
Diesel	£1.11 per litre
Super petrol	£1.17 per litre

    b   The next time he fills his bike it takes 6.3 litres. How much did she pay?

Round all your answers to the nearest penny.

    c   Lucy puts 9.5 litres of diesel into her car. How much did she pay?

    d   How much will it cost Lucy to fill up her car with 21.3 litres of diesel?

    e   Josh's car uses 7.6 litres of super petrol for every 100 km travelled. How much will it cost him to travel 100 km?

    f   How much will it cost to put 15.25 litres of super petrol into Josh's car?

17 Jenna takes this floor plan to get some quotes for carpet and vinyl floor covering.

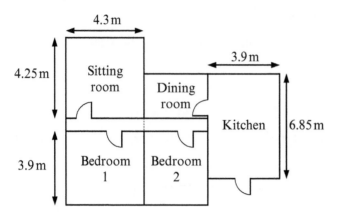

a What area of vinyl will the kitchen need?

b What area of carpet will she need for bedroom 1 and the sitting room combined?

c Carpet costs £15.30 per square metre.

How much will carpet cost for the sitting room and bedroom 1?

explanation 4a   explanation 4b   explanation 4c

18 Work out these divisions.

a 840 ÷ 15	**b** 1848 ÷ 12	**c** 2052 ÷ 18	**d** 2512 ÷ 16
e 1512 ÷ 24	**f** 9630 ÷ 45	**g** 4224 ÷ 32	**h** 3634 ÷ 23
i 3538 ÷ 29	**j** 8160 ÷ 32		

19 How much would each person get if the following amounts of money were shared equally?

a £202.30 shared between 7 people

b £188.32 shared between 8 people

c £189.80 shared between 13 people

d £174.02 shared between 11 people

e £1104.60 shared between 21 people

f £8162.40 shared between 24 people

20 Is A, B, C or D equivalent to the given calculation?

a $94 \div 3.4$

   A $94 \div 34$ B $940 \div 3.4$ C $940 \div 34$ D $9400 \div 34$

b $386 \div 7.9$

   A $386 \div 79$ B $3860 \div 7.9$ C $3860 \div 79$ D $38\,600 \div 79$

c $472 \div 4.6$

   A $4720 \div 46$ B $472 \div 46$ C $47\,200 \div 46$ D $4720 \div 4.6$

d $372.4 \div 5.6$

   A $3724 \div 5.6$ B $3724 \div 56$ C $37\,240 \div 56$ D $37\,240 \div 5.6$

e $12.56 \div 0.55$

   A $125.6 \div 55$ B $1256 \div 5.5$ C $12\,560 \div 55$ D $1256 \div 55$

21 Work these out.

a $117 \div 2.6$ b $378 \div 4.2$ c $425 \div 1.7$ d $238 \div 2.8$

e $145 \div 2.5$ f $144 \div 1.6$ g $189 \div 0.9$ h $212 \div 0.4$

22 How many of each item of clothing can be made from these lengths of fabric?

a   Dresses that use 2 m of fabric from a 32.5 m length.

b   Shorts that use 1.4 m of fabric from a 47.6 m length.

c   Jackets that use 2.1 m of fabric from a 117.6 m length.

d   Skirts that use 1.6 m of fabric from a 353.6 m length.

e   Belts that use 0.13 m of fabric from a 6.76 m length.

23 There are three deals for concession tickets at a gym.

Deal A	Deal B	Deal C
12 tickets for £31.80	25 tickets for £63.75	48 tickets for £114.24

Which is the best deal?

24 Dean's car used 34.6 litres of petrol to travel to Scotland.

On average his car travelled 12.2 km per litre of petrol.

How many kilometres did he travel?

25 A carton containing packets of biscuits weighs 4.5 kg.

The carton weighs 0.9 kg.

If each packet of biscuits weighs 0.4 kg, how many packets of biscuits does the carton hold?

explanation 5

26 These are the prices for vegetables on a market stall.

Potatoes	£1.45 per kg
Cabbages	49p each
Beans	£3.78 per kg
Carrots	£1.70 per kg
Cauliflower	79p each

a   Mrs Graham buys 3 kg potatoes, 1.5 kg beans and a cauliflower.

How much does she pay for her vegetables?

b   Mr Yates buys 2 cabbages, 5 kg potatoes and 2 kg carrots.

How much more does he pay for his shopping than Mrs Graham?

27 a   Dipak bought a new computer on hire purchase.

He made a deposit of £650 and paid the rest off at £62.50 per month for 24 months.

How much did the computer cost him?

b   His friend bought the same computer but his hire purchase deal was for 12 months.

He made a deposit of £980 and paid £78.80 per month.

How much less did he pay for the computer?

28 Rita has to save £1402.20 for her summer holiday.

She has 38 weeks to save the money.

She wants to save the same amount each week. How much will this be?

29 Eight friends go out for a meal. The bill came to £117.20.

    a How much would they each pay if they shared the costs equally?

    b Two friends had more expensive meals so paid £17.50 each.

       The rest shared the remaining bill. How much did they each have to pay?

30 A holiday rental cottage costs €615 per week (7-day rental period).

    a How much does it cost to rent the cottage per day?

    b Linen is charged extra at €12.25 per day.

       What is the total cost of renting the cottage and linen for 4 days?

31 These are the photo processing charges for two firms.

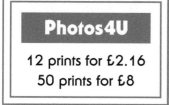

    a Which two deals work out at the same price per print?

    b Which deal gives the most expensive price per print?

32 Sumit had £89 in his bank account.

    a He bought three shirts that cost £23.95 each.

       How much did he have left in his account?

    b The next week the shop had a sale.

       Sumit worked out that he could have bought
five shirts for exactly £89 in the sale.

       How much did the shirts cost in the sale?

Calculator methods

- Using a calculator to solve a wide range of calculations and problems
- Rounding and estimating when using a calculator
- Using the fraction key
- Using a calculator for conversions, such as exchange rates and time

Keywords

You should know

explanation 1a | explanation 1b | explanation 1c | explanation 1d

1 Use the bracket keys on your calculator to work these out.

a $(4.8 - 3.2) \times 12.8$

b $-14.3 \times (1.2 + 2.3)$

c $(43.8 + 26.1) \div 3$

d $(4.6 - 2.9) \times (2.5 + 1.8)$

e $(3.7 + -6.3) \times (7.6 - 3.9)$

f $(4.5 + 6.2) \times (3.8 - 1.75)$

g $7.6 \times (4.35 - 3.72) + -5.83$

h $-18.6 \times (3.4 \div 1.2)$

i $5.6 + 3.8(2.7 + 5.2)$

j $11.8 - 3(3.5 \times 0.4) + 23.5$

2 Conor keyed $\dfrac{14 + 7}{5 - 2}$ as

$$\boxed{1}\ \boxed{4}\ \boxed{+}\ \boxed{7}\ \boxed{\div}\ \boxed{(}\ \boxed{5}\ \boxed{-}\ \boxed{2}\ \boxed{)}\ \boxed{=}$$

His answer of 16.33 (to 2.d.p.) is wrong.

What mistake did Conor make?

3 Use bracket keys correctly to work out these.

If necessary, round your final answer to two decimal places.

a $\dfrac{89 + 56}{47 - 19}$

b $\dfrac{69}{4 \times 5}$

c $\dfrac{73 - 11}{45 - 38}$

d $\dfrac{134 - 18}{2 \times 12}$

e $\dfrac{4.8 + 2.4}{5.9}$

f $\dfrac{3 \times 7.3}{2.9 + 3.7}$

g $\dfrac{2.3 + 2 \times 9}{1.8 \times 2.8}$

h $\dfrac{6.3 \times 4.2}{3.6 \times 8.1}$

i $\dfrac{2 \times 4.7 + 3.7}{1.7 \times 2.9}$

j $\dfrac{3.4 \times 4.6 \times 6.2}{18.4 - 9.5}$

k $\dfrac{34.8 - 6.1 \times 0.5}{4.3 + 2.9}$

4 Find the answers to these correct to 2 d.p.

    a $45.3 \div 3.5 + 4.7 \times 2.6$ **b** $34.6 \times 2.4 - 7.6 \div 0.5$

    c $3.1 \div 1.4 \times 2.6 + 9.6$ **d** $62.1 \div 3.5 - 42.4 \div 3.4$

5 Sandy posted a parcel of presents to her sister's family for Christmas.

The cardboard box and packaging weighed 0.35 kg.

The parcel contained

three 0.850 kg jars of sweets   two jerseys weighing 1.3 kg each

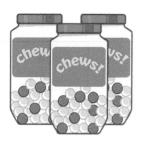 

4 packs of coloured pencils at   3 sets of DVDs weighing
0.675 kg each   0.328 kg each

    a How much did Sandy's parcel weigh?

    b Postage costs £7.50 for the first 5 kg plus £1.42 per kilogram for any weight
over that.

        How much did it cost to post the parcel?

explanation 2a   explanation 2b

6 Use the appropriate keys on your calculator to work these out.

Round your answers to two decimal places where necessary.

a 4^2

b 6^3

c $(-7)^2$

d 1.5^3

e 3.2^5

f $4^4 + (-3)^2$

g $1.3^3 \times 3.7^2$

h $(1.4 + 5.6)^2$

i $\dfrac{6.1^2}{2.4^2}$

j $\dfrac{(2.8 + 5.5)^3}{2.4 + 1.7^2}$

k $\dfrac{5.8^4 - 2.5}{(2.3 + 0.7)^2}$

l $\dfrac{(3.2 - 0.5)^2}{0.9^2 + 2.4}$

7 a Use your calculator to work these out.

  i $1.2^2 \times 1.2^3$

  ii $7.8^2 \times 7.8^3$

  iii $3.4^2 \times 3.4^3$

  iv $4.7^2 \times 4.7^3$

> Do not round
> your answers.

b What do you notice about the last digits in the numbers multiplied together in part **a** and the last digits in the answers?

c What would you expect the last digits of $3.3^2 \times 3.3^3$ and $9.5^2 \times 9.5^3$ to be?

Check with your calculator to see if you are correct.

8 Find the volume of each cube. Give your answers to 2 d.p.

a

b

c

4.8 cm

2.19 cm

13.67 m

9 Use the appropriate keys on your calculator to work these out.

Round your answers to two decimal places where necessary.

a $\sqrt{34}$

b $\sqrt{18.6}$

c $\sqrt[3]{45}$

d $\sqrt[3]{56.8}$

e $\sqrt[5]{81}$

f $\sqrt[4]{48.3}$

g $\sqrt{3.4} + 14.8$

h $\sqrt[3]{65.3} + 23.2$

i $\sqrt{11.5} - 4.7$

j $\sqrt[3]{72.5} + 5.6^2$

k $\sqrt[3]{105.6} - \sqrt{12}$

10 Shona worked out that $\sqrt{25 + 6.8} = 11.8$

Winston worked out that $\sqrt{25 + 6.8} = 5.64$ (to 2 d.p.)

a Why are their answers different?

b Work these out.

   i $\sqrt{56.3 - 23.1}$ ii $\sqrt{3.7 \times 18.6}$ iii $\sqrt{43.2 \div 12.5}$

11 Sachim is tiling a patio.

The area of the patio is $30.625\,\text{m}^2$ and he will need 250 square tiles.

How long is the side of one of the tiles? Give your answer in centimetres.

$1\,\text{m}^2 = 10\,000\,\text{cm}^2$

---

explanation 3

---

12 Work these out using the fraction key on your calculator.

a $\dfrac{3}{7} + \dfrac{5}{9}$ b $1\dfrac{1}{2} - \dfrac{3}{5}$ c $\dfrac{4}{9} \times \dfrac{12}{15}$

d $6\dfrac{4}{11} \times 3\dfrac{1}{3}$ e $\dfrac{6}{7} \div \dfrac{5}{14}$ f $3\dfrac{2}{7} \div 1\dfrac{1}{2}$

g $\dfrac{5}{6} + \dfrac{11}{15} \times \dfrac{1}{2}$ h $9\dfrac{3}{4} \times 1\dfrac{2}{5} \div \dfrac{3}{7}$ i $\dfrac{5}{8} \times \left(\dfrac{4}{7} + 1\dfrac{2}{5}\right)$

> If your calculator does not have a fraction key you can use division and the memory keys or use a written method. Check how you add, subtract, multiply and divide fractions first.

13 The local store did a stocktake of their boxes of Crunchy crisps.

They had these numbers of boxes of the different flavours.

$2\dfrac{2}{3}$ salt and vinegar, $4\dfrac{1}{4}$ cheese and onion,

$3\dfrac{1}{6}$ smoky bacon, $4\dfrac{5}{8}$ chicken and $2\dfrac{5}{6}$ plain

How many boxes was that in total?

14 Convert each of these into days, hours and minutes.

    a 5.6 hours   b 9.9 hours   c 6.25 hours   d 8.75 hours

    e 14.15 hours   f 5.45 hours   g 13.35 hours   h 1.85 hours

    i 0.45 days   j 0.85 days   k 0.1 days   l 2.6 days

    m 5.4 days   n 7.35 days   o 12.45 days   p 6.95 days

15 How long are these times?

    a 10:45 to 12:10   b 09:50 to 11:45   c 11:55 to 17:40

    d 13:34 to 15:21   e 14:57 to 17:35   f 09:12 to 13:07

16 On Monday Mark worked 4.8 hours, on Tuesday 6.7 hours, on Thursday 5.65 hours and on Friday 7.15 hours.

    a How many hours and minutes did he work altogether?

    b At the weekend he worked an additional 0.55 days.

    What was the total number of hours and minutes worked that week?

17 a Use this London to Glasgow train timetable to work out how long these journeys would take.

London Euston		12:35	
Birmingham	11:30		13:26
Preston	13:42	14:48	15:56
Carlisle	14:53	15:05	16:04
Glasgow	16:04		17:23

     i London Euston to Preston

    ii Preston to Glasgow on the 11:30 Birmingham train

  iii Birmingham to Carlisle on the 13:26 Birmingham train

    b Which train is faster, the morning or afternoon Birmingham to Glasgow train?

    By how many minutes?

explanation 5

Use these exchange rates for questions **18** to **23**.

£1 = 1.14 euros (€)

£1 = US$1.45 (US dollars)

£1 = 1.67 Swiss francs

£1 = 9.95 Chinese yuan

£1 = 139.9 Japanese yen

£1 = A$2.24 (Australian dollars)

18 How many pounds would be exchanged for these amounts?

a	€750 (euros)	b	1000 Chinese yuan
c	US$55	d	€348
e	A$230	f	570 Japanese yen
g	250 Swiss francs	h	US$1000

Round all answers
to the nearest £0.01

19 How much in these currencies would be exchanged for £110.50?

Round all answers to two decimal places.

a	euros (€)	b	US dollars	c	Chinese yuan
d	Swiss francs	e	Australian dollars	f	Japanese yen

20 On holiday in Australia, Anna paid A$165.50 per night for her hotel accommodation.

Breakfast cost an extra A$16.80 each day.

a   How much was her bill for three nights' accommodation and breakfast in pounds?

b   She also hired a rental car for the three days at a cost of A$35.40 per day plus a one-off insurance cost of A$56.75.
What was the cost of this in pounds?

21 A bus trip to the Great Wall of China from Beijing cost Peter 65 Chinese yuan.

   a How much did the ticket cost in pounds?

   b Peter bought tickets for six people in his group and received a 5% discount.

     How much did it cost him, in pounds, for the six tickets?

22 Megan saw this advert on the internet.

Buy your favourite DVDs direct from the USA

US$14.95 for each DVD + shipping US$1.99 per DVD

Buy 5 DVDS and each DVD costs US$11.75 + total shipping of US$5.99.

   a How much did Megan pay, in pounds, for three DVDs to be shipped to her?

   b She later ordered another two DVDs.

     What was the total cost in pounds for Megan to get all five DVDs?

   c How much money, in pounds, would she have saved if she had ordered all five DVDs at the same time?

23 When Sara returned from her Swiss skiing trip she took 214 Swiss francs into her bank to change back into pounds.

   a How many pounds would she have expected to get?

   b Sara got less than she expected as the bank charged 3% for changing her money.

     How much did Sara actually get?

Sequences

- Generating a sequence from a term–to–term rule
- Generating a sequence from a position–to–term rule
- Finding the position–to–term rule for a sequence
- Writing a position–to–term rule using algebra

Keywords

You should know

explanation 1

1 Look at each sequence.

a

Position	1	2	3	4	
Term	3	5			

   i Draw the next shape in the pattern.

   ii Copy and complete the sequence table for this pattern.

   iii Describe the term-to-term rule for the sequence.

b

Position	1	2	3	4	
Term	1	5			

   i Draw the next two shapes in the pattern.

   ii Copy and complete the sequence table for this pattern.

   iii Describe the term-to-term rule for the sequence.

c

Position	1	2	3		
Term	3				

   i Draw the next two shapes in the pattern.

   ii Copy and complete the sequence table for this pattern.

   iii Describe the term-to-term rule for the sequence.

2 Look at each sequence.

    i Write the next two terms in each sequence.

    ii Describe the term-to-term rule.

a 2, 5, 8, 11, 14   b 6, 8, 10, 12, 14   c 6, 10, 14, 18, 22

d 32, 29, 26, 23, 20   e 8, 13, 18, 23, 28   *f 20, 13, 6, −1, −8

*g 17, 12, 7, 2, −3   *h −26, −21, −16, −11, −6   *i 16, 13, 10, 7, 4

3 Find the first five terms in each sequence.
Use the first term and the term-to-term rule.

	Term-to-term rule	1st term	First five terms
	+ 3	4	4, 7, 10, 13, 16
a	+ 7	1	
b	+ 0.5	3.5	
c	− 4	13	
d	+ 0.5	2.3	
e	− 4	−1	

4 Look at each sequence.

    i Write the missing terms in each sequence.

    ii Describe the term-to-term rule.

a 1, 4, 7, ☐, 13, ☐   b 2, 6, ☐, 14, 18, ☐

c 9, ☐, 13, ☐, 17, 19, ☐   d 3, ☐, 15, ☐, 27, ☐

e 32, 30, ☐, 26, ☐   f 66, ☐, ☐, 33, ☐, 11

g 1, 5, 9, ☐, 17, ☐   h 10, 6, ☐, −2, −6, ☐

*i 1, ☐, 4, 6.5, ☐, 9.5   *j 7, ☐, ☐, ☐, 5, 4.5

*k 96, 48, 24, ☐, 6, ☐   *l ☐, 1, 2, 4, ☐, 16

5 Copy and complete the table.

	Term-to-term rule	1st term	First five terms
a	+ 8	7	☐, ☐, ☐, ☐, ☐
b			☐, 7, 13, 19, 25
c	− 5	12	☐, ☐, ☐, ☐, ☐
d			☐, 12, 6, 0, −6
e	− 4		☐, −5, −9, −13, −17
*f			☐, −8, −3, 2, 7

*6 The term-to-term rule for a sequence is:

If the number is even, divide by 2. If the number is odd, multiply it by 3 and add 1. If the number is 1, stop.

Use this rule to find the 18 terms in this sequence 92, 46, ...

(explanation 2a) (explanation 2b)

7 Look at the function machine.

a Copy and complete the function machine and sequence table.
Use this position-to-term rule:

Term = Position × 5

Position   Term
   1   5
   2   10
   3 → × 5 → ☐
   4   ☐
   5   ☐

Position	1	2	3	4	5
Term	5	10			

b What is the 100th term in this sequence?

c Is 60 in this sequence? Explain how you know.

197

8 Look at the sequence table.

Position	1	2	3	4	5
Term					

    a Copy and complete the sequence table using this position-to-term rule:

        Term = Position + 4

    b What is the 100th term in this sequence?

    *c 20 is a term in the sequence. What is the position of this term? Explain how you know.

9 Look at the function machine and sequence table.

    a Copy and complete the function machine and sequence table using the position-to-term rule: Term = Position × 2 + 3

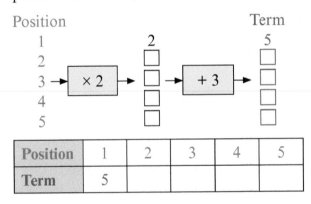

Position	1	2	3	4	5
Term	5				

    b What is the 100th term in this sequence?

    *c 53 is a term in the sequence. What is the position of this term? Explain how you know.

10 Here is a sequence table.

    a Copy and complete the sequence table using this position-to-term rule:

Position	1	2	3	4	5
Term					

        Term = Position × 3 − 2

    b What is the 100th term in this sequence?

    *c 58 is a term in the sequence. What is the position of this term? Explain how you know.

11 Look at each position-to-term rule.

> **i** Copy and complete a sequence table, using the position-to-term rule.

Position	1	2	3	4	5
Term					

> **ii** Work out the 100th term in the sequence.

> **iii** Work out if 32 is a term in the sequence. Explain your answer.

a Term = Position × 5 − 3   **b** Term = Position × 4 + 1

c Term = Position × 6 − 8   **d** Term = Position ÷ 2 + 3

e Term = Position × 2 − 7   **f** Term = (Position + 3) × 2

g Term = Position × 3 − 5   **h** Term = (Position + 8) ÷ 2

i Term = (Position − 1) × 3   **j** Term = (Position ÷ 2) + 0.5

> explanation 3

12 Look at each sequence below.

> **i** Draw the pattern of dots in position 4.

> **ii** Write a position-to-term rule: Number of dots = _____

> **iii** Write your rule, using algebra: D = _____

> **iv** Describe the dot pattern in position 10.

a

Pattern	• •	• • • •	• • • • • •	
Position (n)	1	2	3	4
Number of dots (D)	2	4	6	8

b

Pattern	• • •	• • • • • •	• • • • • • • • •	
Position (n)	1	2	3	4
Number of dots (D)	3	6	9	12

13 Look at each sequence below.

    i Draw the pattern in position 4.

    ii Write a position-to-term rule in words. (Hint: there are two steps.)

    iii Write your rule using algebra.

    iv Describe the pattern in position 10.

a

Pattern				
Position (n)	1	2	3	4
Number of dots (D)	1	4	7	10

b

Pattern				
Position (P)	1	2	3	4
Number of triangles (T)	1	3	5	7

c

Pattern				
Position (P)	1	2	3	4
Number of squares (S)	2	6	10	14

d

Pattern				
Position (P)	1	2	3	4
Number of triangles (T)	2	5	8	11

e

Pattern				
Position (P)	1	2	3	4
Number of stars (S)	1	5	9	13

explanation 4

14 Using algebra, write the rule that links the input and output for each function machine. The function machines have two steps each.
The first one has been done for you.

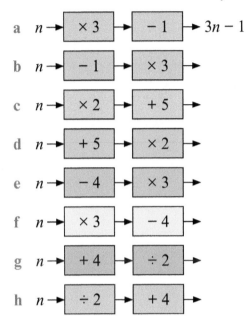

a $n \rightarrow \boxed{\times 3} \rightarrow \boxed{-1} \rightarrow 3n - 1$

b $n \rightarrow \boxed{-1} \rightarrow \boxed{\times 3} \rightarrow$

c $n \rightarrow \boxed{\times 2} \rightarrow \boxed{+5} \rightarrow$

d $n \rightarrow \boxed{+5} \rightarrow \boxed{\times 2} \rightarrow$

e $n \rightarrow \boxed{-4} \rightarrow \boxed{\times 3} \rightarrow$

f $n \rightarrow \boxed{\times 3} \rightarrow \boxed{-4} \rightarrow$

g $n \rightarrow \boxed{+4} \rightarrow \boxed{\div 2} \rightarrow$

h $n \rightarrow \boxed{\div 2} \rightarrow \boxed{+4} \rightarrow$

> If you want to add or subtract before you multiply or divide, you must use brackets.

explanation 5

15 Find the position-to-term rule and the nth term for each sequence.

a $n \rightarrow \boxed{\times \square} \rightarrow \boxed{+ \square} \rightarrow$

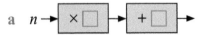

Position (n)	1	2	3	4
Term	5	8	11	14

b $n \rightarrow \boxed{\times \square} \rightarrow \boxed{- \square} \rightarrow$

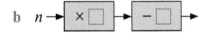

Position (n)	1	2	3	4
Term	−1	1	3	5

c $n \rightarrow \boxed{\square} \rightarrow \boxed{\square} \rightarrow$

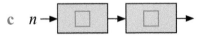

Position (n)	1	2	3	4
Term	2	6	10	14

d $n \rightarrow \boxed{\square} \rightarrow \boxed{\square} \rightarrow$

Position (n)	1	2	3	4
Term	−3	0	3	6

16 Look at each sequence.

   i Find the position-to-term rule.

   ii Find the nth term of the sequence.

   iii Find the 100th term.

a

Position	1	2	3	4	5
Term	6	12	18	24	30

b

Position	1	2	3	4	5
Term	10	15	20	25	30

c

Position	1	2	3	4	5
Term	−4	−2	0	2	4

d

Position	1	2	3	4	5
Term	2	5	8	11	14

e

Position	1	2	3	4	5
Term	2	6	10	14	18

f

Position	1	2	3	4	5
Term	3	9	15	21	27

g

Position	1	2	3	4	5
Term	−4	−1	2	5	8

*17 Look at each matchstick pattern.

> i Draw and complete a sequence table.
>
> ii Find the *n*th term rule for the sequence.
>
> iii How many matchsticks will be in position 100?

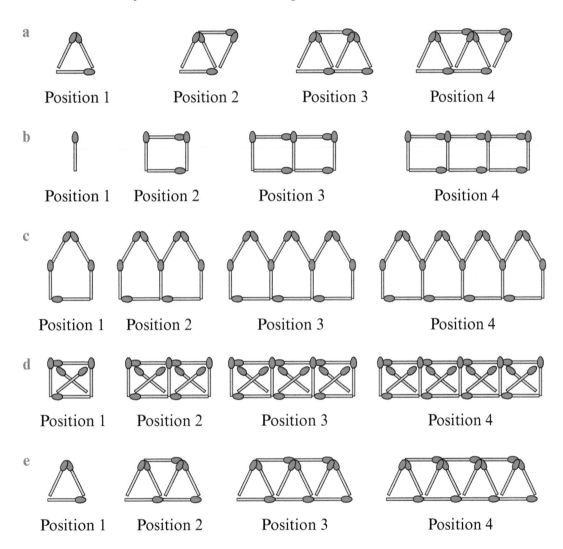

a

Position 1   Position 2   Position 3   Position 4

b

Position 1   Position 2   Position 3   Position 4

c

Position 1   Position 2   Position 3   Position 4

d

Position 1   Position 2   Position 3   Position 4

e

Position 1   Position 2   Position 3   Position 4

*18 Look at your answers to question 17.

Describe how your *n*th term rules are linked to each pattern of matchsticks.

Mappings and straight-line graphs

- Drawing a mapping diagram
- Finding the equation of a line on a coordinate grid
- Finding the equation of a line from coordinates on the line
- Drawing a graph from its equation

Keywords

You should know

explanation 1a   explanation 1b

1 Copy and complete these function machines. Use the mapping given.

a $x \rightarrow x + 3$

1
3 → □ → □
□   10

b $x \rightarrow 4x$

1
5 → □ → □
□   36

c $x \rightarrow x - 1$

2
6 → □ → □
□   9

d $x \rightarrow \dfrac{x}{2}$

4
9 → □ → □
□   8

2 Copy and complete these function machines. Use the mapping given.

a $x \rightarrow 2x + 3$

3
5 → ×2 → +3 → □
10

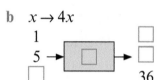

b $x \rightarrow 2(x + 3)$

3
5 → +3 → ×2 → □
10

c $x \rightarrow \dfrac{x}{2} + 4$

4
6 → ÷2 → +4 → □
9

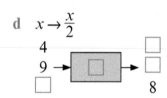

d $x \rightarrow \dfrac{(x + 4)}{2}$

4
6 → +4 → ÷2 → □
9

e $x \rightarrow 3x - 1$

2
7 → □ → □ → □
8

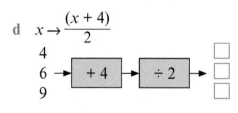

f $x \rightarrow 3(x - 1)$

2
7 → □ → □ → □
8

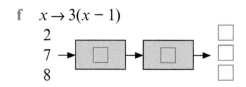

explanation 2

3 In these questions, mappings are given using algebra.

    i Write each mapping as a function machine. The first one has been done for you.

    ii Copy and complete each table.

    iii Copy and complete each mapping diagram.

a $x \to x + 2$

$x \to \boxed{+2} \to y$

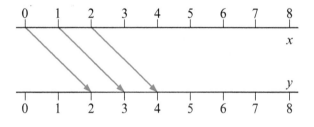

Input	Output
0	2
1	3
2	4
3	
4	
5	

b $x \to 2x$

$x \to \boxed{\ \square\ } \to y$

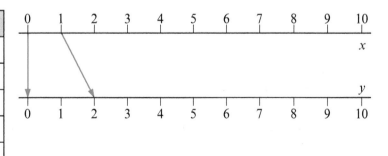

Input	Output
0	0
1	2
2	
3	
4	
5	

4 In these questions, mappings are given using algebra.

    i Write each mapping as a function machine. The first one has been done for you.

    ii Copy and complete each table.

    iii Copy and complete each mapping diagram.

a $x \rightarrow 2x - 2$

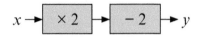

Input	Output
1	
2	
3	4
4	
5	

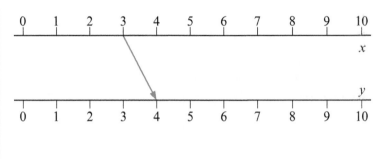

b $x \rightarrow 2(x - 2)$

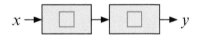

Input	Output
1	
2	0
3	
4	
5	

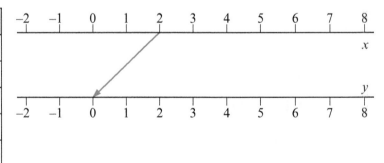

5 Copy and complete this mapping diagram for each function.

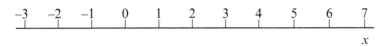

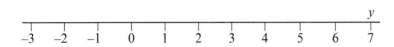

a $x \rightarrow 3x - 2$ for $x = 0, 1, 2, 3$

b $x \rightarrow 3(x - 2)$ for $x = 1, 2, 3, 4$

c $x \rightarrow 2(x - 1)$ for $x = 0, 1, 2, 3, 4$

d $x \rightarrow 2x - 1$ for $x = -1, 0, 1, 2, 3, 4$

> **explanation 3**

6 The diagram shows two straight lines.

  a Write the coordinates of each of the points A to F.

  b Write the equation of the line that goes through points A, B, C and D.

  c Write the equation of the line that goes through points B, E and F.

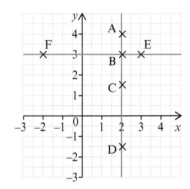

7 The graph shows six straight lines marked (a) to (f).

  a Match each line to its equation to leave two equations left over.

$y = -2$	$x = -2$
$y = 4$	$x = 4$
$y = 1$	$x = 1$
$y = 2$	$x = 2$

  b Draw a diagram to show the graphs that match the two remaining equations.

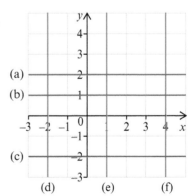

You may find it helpful to sketch diagrams when answering questions **8** to **10**.

8 **a** Write the equation of the line through (2, 5) and (−4, 5).

   b Write the equation of the line through (−3, 4) and (−3, −1).

   c Write the coordinates of the point where the two lines cross.

9 **a** Write the coordinates of the point where the lines $x = 7$ and $y = 3$ cross.

   b Write the equations of two lines that cross at (1, 2).

   c Write the coordinates of the point where the lines $x = -3$ and $y = 4$ cross.

   d Write the equations of two lines that cross at (−6, −1).

*10 **a** Explain why the equation of the y-axis is $x = 0$.

   b What is the equation of the x-axis?

> **explanation 4**

11 The graph shows four points A, B, C and D on a straight line.

   a Copy this table. Use the four points to complete it.

Point	x	y
A	4	3
B		
C		
D		

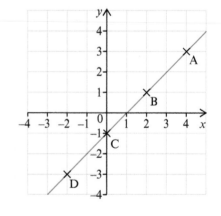

   b Describe the link between the y-coordinate and the x-coordinate of any point on the line.

   c Copy and complete this rule. $x \longrightarrow \boxed{} \longrightarrow y$

   d Write the equation of the line. $y = $ _____

12 The graph shows four points A, B, C and D on a straight line.

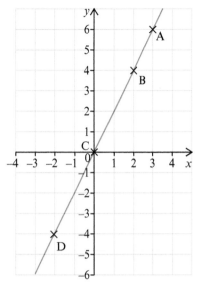

a   Copy this table. Use the four points to complete it.

Point	x	y
A	3	6
B		
C		
D		

b   Describe the link between the y-coordinate and the x-coordinate of any point on the line.

c   Copy and complete the rule. $x \rightarrow \boxed{} \rightarrow y$

d   Write the equation of the line. $y = $ _____

13 The graph shows four points A, B, C and D on a straight line.

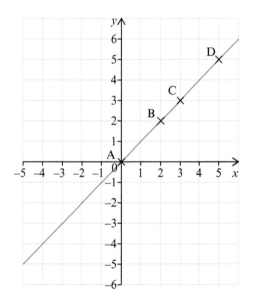

a   Copy this table. Use the four points to complete it.

Point	x	y
A	0	0
B		
C		
D		

b   What do you notice about the x-coordinate and the y-coordinate of any point on the line?

c   Write the equation of the line. $y = $ _____

14 The graph shows four points A, B, C and D on a straight line.

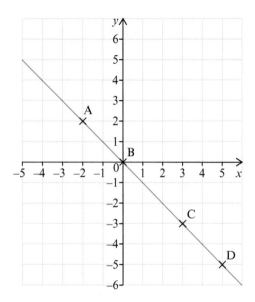

a Copy this table. Use the four points to complete it.

Point	x	y
A	−2	2
B		
C		
D		

b What do you notice about the x-coordinate and the y-coordinate of any point on the line?

c Write the equation of the line. $y =$ _____

explanation 5

15 This question is about the line with equation $y = x + 5$.

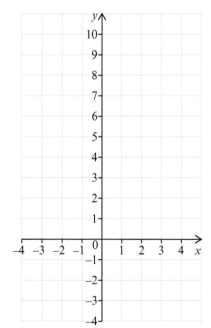

a Copy and complete the table for points on the line.

Point	x	y
A	−1	
B	0	
C	1	
D	2	

b Copy the axes and plot the points from your table.

c Draw a line through your points to the edge of the grid. Label the line with its equation.

16 This question is about the line with equation $y = x - 3$.

a Copy and complete the table for points on the line.

Point	x	y
A	−1	
B	0	
C	1	
D	2	

b Copy the axes and plot the points from your table.

c Draw a line through your points to the edge of the grid. Label the line with its equation.

17 Repeat question **16** for the line with equation $y = 3x$.

18 Repeat question **16** for the line with equation $y = \frac{1}{2}x$.

explanation 6a   explanation 6b

19 In the line with equation $x + y = 3$, the x-coordinate and the y-coordinate of each point always add to 3.

a Copy and complete the table for points on the line.

Point	x	y
A	−1	
B	0	
C	1	
D	2	

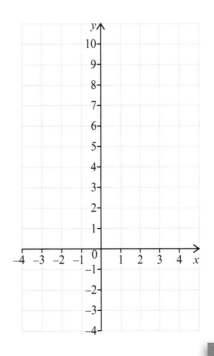

b Copy the axes and plot the points from your table.

c Draw a line through your points to the edge of the grid. Label the line with its equation.

20 Repeat question **19** for the line with equation $x + y = 1$.

***21** Repeat question **19** for the line with equation $x + y = -2$.

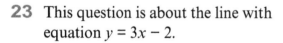

explanation 7

22 This question is about the line with equation $y = 2x + 3$.

    a Copy and complete the table for points on the line.

Point	x	y
A	0	
B	1	
C	2	
D	3	

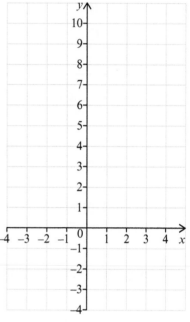

    b Copy the axes and plot the points from your table.

    c Draw a line through your points to the edge of the grid. Label the line with its equation.

23 This question is about the line with equation $y = 3x - 2$.

    a Copy and complete the table for points on the line.

Point	x	y
A	0	
B	1	
C	2	
D	3	

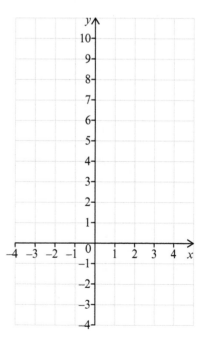

    b Copy the axes and plot the points from your table.

    c Draw a line through your points to the edge of the grid. Label the line with its equation.

24 Repeat question **23** for the line with equation $y = 4x - 3$.

25 Repeat question **23** for the line with equation $y = 2x - 5$.

*26 In the line with equation $y = 10 - 2x$, the y-coordinate is double the x-coordinate subtracted from 10.

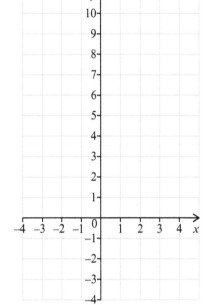

a Copy and complete the table for points on the line.

Point	x	y
A	0	
B	1	
C	2	
D	3	

b Copy the axes and plot the points from your table.

c Draw a line through your points to the edge of the grid. Label the line with its equation.

*27 Repeat question **26** for the line with equation $y = 8 - 2x$.

*28 Repeat question **26** for the line with equation $y = 6 - 3x$.

*29 Look back at the different graphs you drew in this section and compare them to their equations.

a Which part of the equation of the graph tells you where the line crosses the y-axis?

b Which part of the equation of the graph tells you about the direction and steepness of the line?

Using graphs

- Using a graph to convert one quantity into another
- Drawing graphs based on real situations
- Interpreting distance–time graphs

Keywords

You should know

explanation 1

1 You can use this graph to convert between pounds (lb) and kilograms (kg).

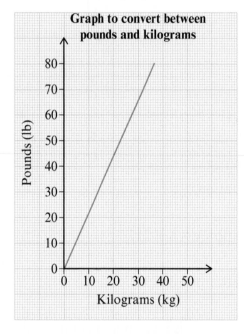

Graph to convert between pounds and kilograms

a   Use the graph to work out approximately how many pounds are in these.

i 20 kg   ii 35 kg

b   Use the graph to work out approximately how many kilograms are in these.

i 30 lb   ii 67 lb

c   Explain how you can use the graph to work out how many pounds are in 200 kg.

2 You can use this graph to convert between temperatures in degrees Celsius (°C) and degrees Fahrenheit (°F).

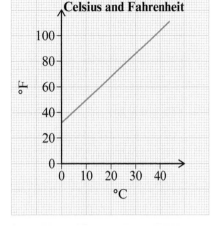

Graph to convert between Celsius and Fahrenheit

a   Use the graph to write these temperatures in degrees Fahrenheit.

  i 15°C   ii 30°C

b   Use the graph to write these temperatures in degrees Celsius.

  i 50°F   ii 90°F

c   Water boils at 100°C.

  Paul says that because 20°C = 68°F, then 100°C = 68°F × 5 = 340°F.

  What feature of the graph tells you that this method will not be correct?

3   The table shows equivalent distances in miles and kilometres.

a   Using the conversion 10 miles to 16 kilometres, copy and complete the table.

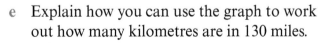

Number of miles	0	10	20	30	40	50
Number of kilometres	0	16		48		

b   Copy these axes. Use the table to draw a conversion graph between miles and kilometres.

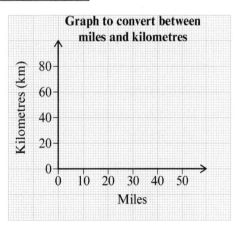

Graph to convert between miles and kilometres

c   Use the graph to work out these distances to the nearest kilometre.

  i 15 miles   ii 27 miles

d   Use the graph to work out these distances to the nearest mile.

  i 8 km   ii 20 km

e   Explain how you can use the graph to work out how many kilometres are in 130 miles.

4 A mobile phone company charges a £10 monthly fee and then £0.05 per minute for calls. The table shows the cost of using their mobile for different amounts of time per month.

Number of minutes	0	60	120	180	240	300
Cost (£)	10	13	16	19	22	25

   a Draw a set of axes. Show the number of minutes on the *x*-axis, using a scale of 10 squares to 60 minutes. Show the cost on the *y*-axis, using a scale of 10 squares to £1.

   b Use the values in the table to plot the conversion graph.

   c Use your graph to work out approximately how much you would be charged in 1 month for these total call times.

     i 30 minutes   **ii** 45 minutes   **iii** $2\frac{1}{2}$ hours

   d Use your graph to work out approximately how long you would have spent on calls in 1 month for these total costs.

     i £14.50   **ii** £20   **iii** £24

   *e Paul said: '3 hours costs £19, so 6 hours will cost £38 because it will be double.'

     Explain why Paul is not correct.

> explanation 2

5 The graph shows a distance–time graph of a car travelling at a constant speed.

   a How far did the car travel in 10 minutes?

   b How long did it take to travel 15 miles?

   c How far did the car travel in $\frac{1}{2}$ hour?

   d The car continued travelling at the same speed for a further $\frac{1}{2}$ hour.

     How far did it travel?

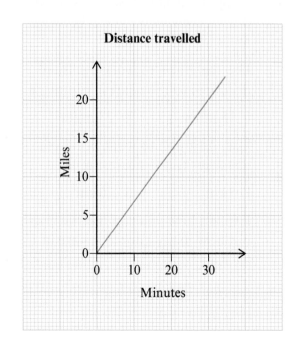

Distance travelled

6 The graph shows a distance–time graph of Mrs Smith's journey to take her son, Ben, and his friend, Alex, to school.

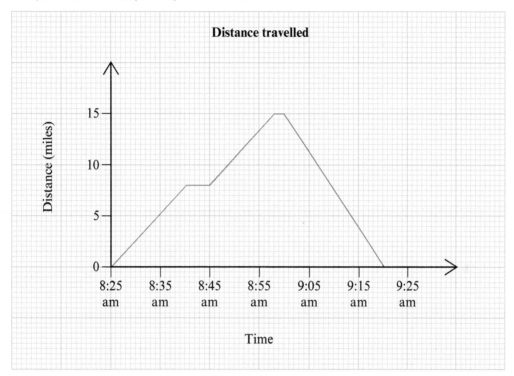

Distance travelled

a   How far is Alex's house from Ben's house?

b   How long did it take to get there?

c   How long did Mrs Smith stop at Alex's house?

d   What time did they arrive at school?

e   How long did the journey home take Mrs Smith?

f   How far did Mrs Smith travel altogether?

7 The distance–time graph shows Martin's journey on a stretch of the motorway.

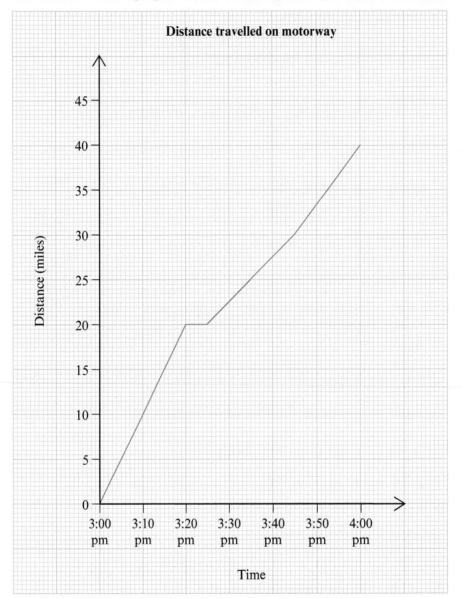

Distance travelled on motorway

a   At what time did Martin get stuck in a traffic jam on the motorway?

b   How far had he travelled by then?

c   For how long was the traffic stationary?

d   How far did Martin travel between 3 pm and 4 pm?

e   Between what times did Martin travel the fastest?

How can you tell this from the graph?

8   The distance–time graph shows Amy's journey by car.

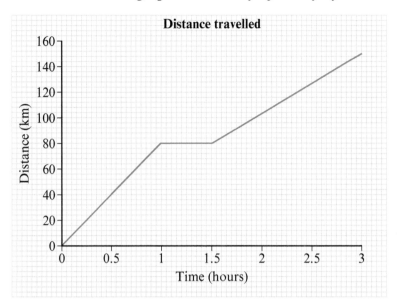

a   How far had Amy travelled after 30 minutes?

b   How long did it take Amy to travel 60 km?

c   Amy stopped for lunch during her journey. How long did she stop for?

d   How far did Amy travel after her lunch until she reached her destination?

9   Sarah and Charlotte live 6 miles apart.
Sarah lives nearer to town than Charlotte.
They are going to meet in town.
Sarah cycles into town and Charlotte catches
the bus.
The distance–time graph shows their journey.

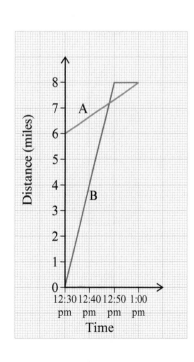

a   Which line represents Sarah on her bicycle
and which line represents Charlotte on the
bus? Explain how you know.

b   What time did Charlotte arrive in town?

c   How long was Charlotte's bus journey?

d   At what time approximately does Charlotte's
bus overtake Sarah?

e   How long did Charlotte have to wait in town
to meet Sarah?

3-D shapes

- Identifying 3-D shapes
- Drawing a 2-D representation of a 3-D shape, using isometric paper
- Identifying the plan and elevations of a 3-D shape
- Drawing the plan and elevations of a 3-D shape

Keywords

You should know

explanation 1a explanation 1b explanation 1c

1 Match each shape to its label.

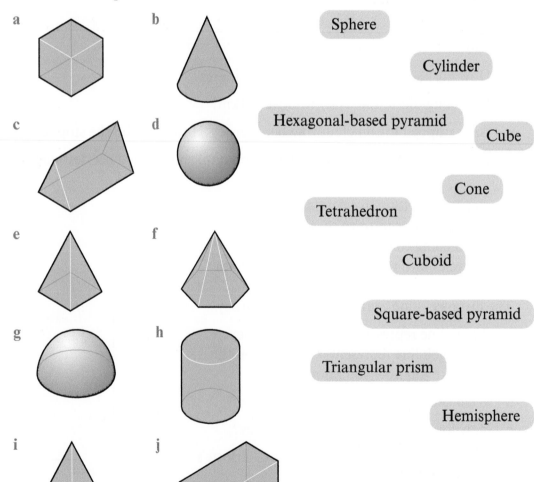

a b

Sphere

Cylinder

c d

Hexagonal-based pyramid

Cube

Cone

Tetrahedron

e f

Cuboid

Square-based pyramid

g h

Triangular prism

Hemisphere

i j

2   The diagram shows a cuboid.
Two corners have been cut off.

How many faces, vertices and edges
does the shape have now?

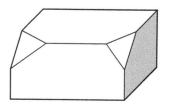

explanation 2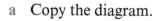

3   This diagram shows six cubes drawn on isometric
dotted paper. They make a 2-D representation of a
cuboid that has length 3 units, width 2 units and
height 1 unit.

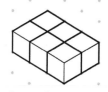

   a   Copy the diagram.

   b   Add another layer of cubes to make a 2-D representation of a cuboid that
has length 3 units, width 2 units and height 2 units.

4   This diagram shows four cubes drawn on
isometric dotted paper.

   a   Copy the diagram.

   b   Add another layer of cubes to make a
2-D representation of a cube that has
length 2 units, width 2 units and height 2 units.

5   This diagram shows three cubes drawn on
isometric dotted paper.

   a   Copy the diagram and add 2 extra cubes to make a
2-D representation of a capital letter L.

   b   Copy the diagram and add 3 extra cubes to make a
2-D representation of the capital letter T.

6   Use isometric dotted paper to draw a 2-D representation of each shape.

   a   A cube of length 3 units, width 3 units and height 3 units

   b   A cuboid of length 3 units, width 2 units and height 4 units

   c   A capital letter I made from 8 cubes

   d   A capital letter F made from 9 cubes

221

7 Match each plan and side elevation (from the right) with the shapes below.

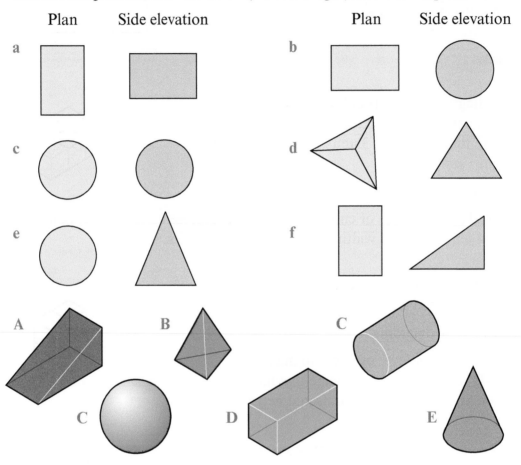

8 Draw the plan and side elevation (from the right) for each shape.

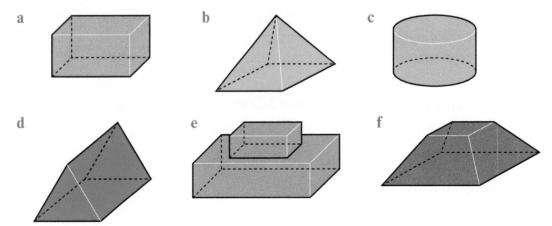

explanation 4

9 The diagram shows a 3-D shape and its plan and elevations.

Which diagram shows these?

    i the plan

    ii the front elevation

    iii the side elevation from the right

    iv the side elevation from the left

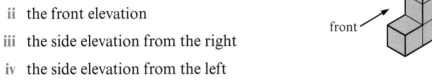
front

a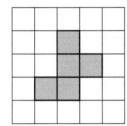

b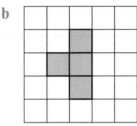

c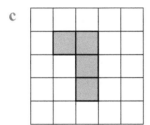

d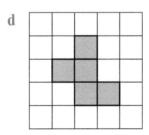

10 Draw the plan, front elevation and both side elevations of each shape.

a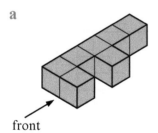
front

b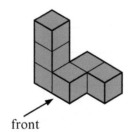
front

c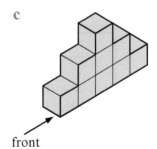
front

11 Draw the plan, front elevation and both side elevations of each shape.

a   b   c

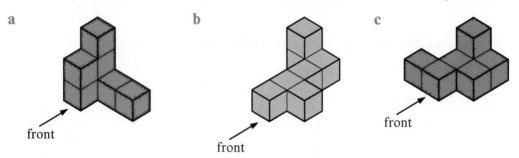

*12 The diagrams show the plan, front elevation and side elevations of four 3-D shapes.

Draw each 3-D shape on isometric dotted paper.

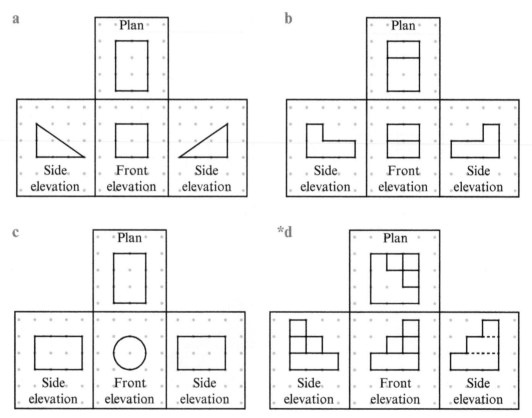

Measures

- Reading scales on a variety of instruments
- Approximating sizes of everyday objects in metric units
- Converting between different metric units
- Recognising common imperial units
- Converting between common imperial and metric units

explanation 1

1 Measure the length of each line.
Give your answers in centimetres to the nearest millimetre.

a ———————————————————————

b —————————————————————————

c ————————————————

d ——————————————————————

e ——————————————

2 Write the value at each lettered point on these scales.

a 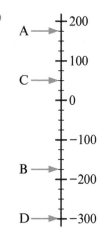 b 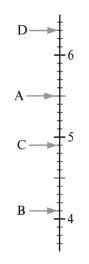 c d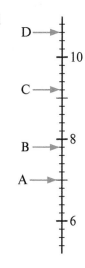

3 The temperature in a house is controlled by a thermostat.

Find the temperature set on the thermostat.

4 Read the values shown on these instruments. Remember to include the units.

a
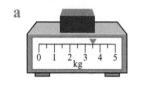

b

c
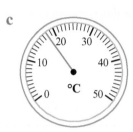

d

e

5 The diagram shows part of a tape measure.

The tape measure is being used to measure the width of a calculator.

Write the width of the calculator.
Use these units.

a centimetres

b inches

6 The diagram shows the speedometer of a car.

The speed of a car can be measured in miles per hour or kilometres per hour.

Write the speed shown on the speedometer.
Use these units.

a kilometres per hour (km/h)

b miles per hour (mph)

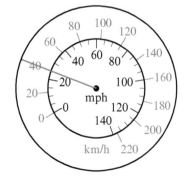

explanation 2

7 Write the times shown on the clocks.

   i Write them as 12-hour clock times.

   ii Write them as 24-hour clock times.

a    b    c    d

morning   morning   afternoon   evening

8 Write these as 24-hour clock times.

   a 6:05 p.m.   **b** 4:22 p.m.   **c** 9:20 a.m.

   d 11:30 a.m.   **e** 11:55 p.m.   **f** 10:42 a.m.

   g 3:45 a.m.   **h** 2:35 p.m.   **i** 12:15 a.m.

9 Write these as 12-hour clock times.

   a 07:21   **b** 15:20   **c** 22:24

   d 17:15   **e** 01:09   **f** 13:36

   g 08:25   **h** 20:45   **i** 00:03

10 At Steven's school, morning break starts at 10:20 a.m.

   It lasts for 15 minutes. What time does it finish?

11 Peter catches the bus to school at 8:15 a.m.

   He arrives at school at 8:40 a.m. How long was his journey?

12 Sally started queuing for the clothes
   shop sale at 4:45 a.m.

   The shop opened at 6:30 a.m.

   How long did Sally queue for?

13 Danielle went to the cinema. The film started at 3:50 p.m. and finished at 6:05 p.m. How long was the film?

14 Craig started his homework at 4:25 p.m. and finished at 6:15 p.m.

How long did he spend on his homework?

15 Deborah went jogging this morning. She left her house at 6:45 a.m. and returned at 7:20 a.m. How long was she out jogging?

16 Harry started working in the garden at 10:50 a.m. and stopped for a break at 12:35 p.m. How long had he been working in the garden?

17 The school bus leaves the bus station at 07:18 and returns at 09:43. How long is the bus away from the station?

18 Margaret is travelling from Nottingham to Birmingham and has to change trains at Leicester. Her arrival time at Leicester is 09:53 and her departure time is 10:16.

How long does Margaret have to wait at Leicester?

19 Ian's train to Sheffield leaves King's Cross station at 15:39.

a   The train is due to reach Chesterfield after 2 hours and 8 minutes.

What time will this be?

b   The train is due to arrive at Sheffield at 18:04.

How long will Ian's train journey be?

explanation 3

20 The tables below show part of a timetable of train services between London and Plymouth.

London Paddington	0857	0957	1057	1127
Reading	0932	1032	1132	1202
Taunton	1059	1156	1247	1341
Tiverton Parkway	1112			1355
Exeter St Davids	1129	1226	1314	1412
Plymouth	1232	1333	1414	

Plymouth	1500	1600	1657	1800
Exeter St Davids	1600	1700	1800	1905
Tiverton Parkway	1616	1716	1816	1920
Taunton	1630	1730	1830	1935
Reading	1751	1851	2007	2051
London Paddington	1821	1924	2039	2121

a   i What time does the train that leaves London Paddington at 09:57 arrive at Taunton?

   ii How long does the journey last?

b   i How long does the 10:57 train from London Paddington take to travel to Plymouth?

   ii If the train is delayed for 8 minutes between Exeter and Plymouth, what time will it arrive in Plymouth?

c   i Jennifer wants to travel from Reading to Taunton.
       She needs to arrive at Taunton before 12 p.m.
       What is the latest train she should catch from Reading?

   ii How long will her train journey be?

d   i Paul wants to travel from Reading to Exeter to attend a conference.
       He catches the train that leaves London Paddington at 08:57.
       How long will his journey be?

   ii He wants to arrive back in Reading between 8 p.m. and 9 p.m.
       What trains could he catch from Exeter St Davids?

explanation 4a   explanation 4b

21 Look at each picture.

    i Which unit would be the most sensible to measure the length in real life?

    ii Estimate the real-life length.

a

b

c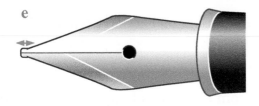

d

e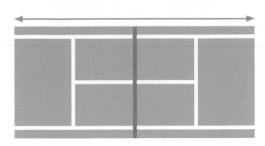

f

22 Copy and complete the table.

Measurement in cm and mm	Measurement in mm	Measurement in cm
6 cm 5 mm		
	85 mm	
		3.6 cm
	234 mm	
2 cm 8 mm		

23 Copy and complete these.

    a 8 cm = ☐ mm   **b** 45 mm = ☐ cm   **c** 9.5 cm = ☐ mm

    d 4.6 cm = ☐ mm   **e** 830 mm = ☐ cm   **f** 12 mm = ☐ cm

    g 146 cm = ☐ m   **h** 2.7 m = ☐ cm   **i** 483 mm = ☐ m

24 Work out which measurement is bigger. Give a reason for each answer.

  a 28 mm, 3 cm   b 9.3 cm, 870 mm   c 26 cm, 0.32 m

  d 0.75 m, 280 mm   e 48.2 cm, 630 mm   f 512 mm, 0.4 m

25 Use these lengths for this question.

  43 cm 8 mm, 5.4 m, 380 mm, 0.5 m, 960 mm

  a Change the measurements so that they are all in centimetres.

  b Use your answer to part **a** to put the original lengths in order of size.
     Start with the longest.

26 Put these lengths in order of size. Start with the longest.

  a 135 cm, 84 mm, 1.4 m, 0.85 m, 860 mm, 8 cm 5 mm

  b 230 mm, 0.3 m, 32 cm, 120 mm, 0.06 m, 44 cm 6 mm

> (explanation 5a) (explanation 5b)

27 Match these items to their labels.

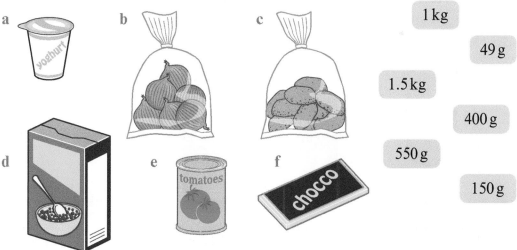

28 Copy and complete these.

  a 3000 g = ☐ kg   b 1.5 kg = ☐ g   c 500 g = ☐ kg

  d 0.8 kg = ☐ g   e 0.03 kg = ☐ g   f 650 g = ☐ kg

  g 2250 g = ☐ kg   h 1.25 kg = ☐ g   i 8.2 kg = ☐ g

  j 0.3 kg = ☐ g   k 20 g = ☐ kg   l 0.05 kg = ☐ g

29 Put these quantities in order of size. Start with the largest.

    a   1 kg, 495 g, 0.85 kg, 2000 g, 0.06 kg

    b   0.5 kg, 650 g, 1 kg 25 g, 1.2 kg, 3000 g

30 Find the total mass in kilograms of the items in each basket.

31 Anna buys a bag of potatoes. It weighs 3.75 kg. She weighs out 450 g to cook. What is the mass of the potatoes left in the bag?

32 Shaun buys a tub of chocolates. It weighs 1.5 kg.
He gives 345 g to each of his 3 sisters. How much chocolate does he have left?

(explanation 6a)   (explanation 6b)

33 Match these items to their labels.

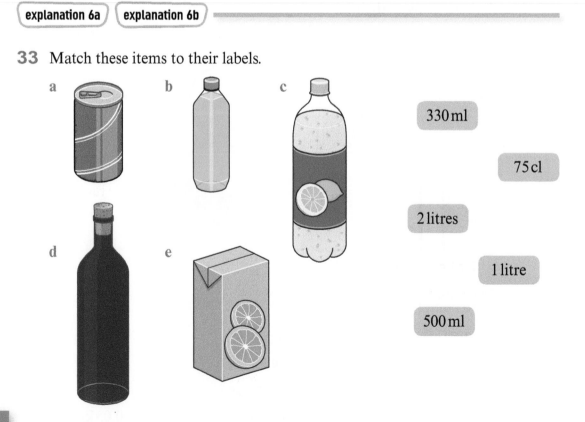

330 ml

75 cl

2 litres

1 litre

500 ml

34 Copy and complete these.

a 75 cl = ☐ litres   b 3.5 litres = ☐ ml   c 30 cl = ☐ litres

d 330 ml = ☐ cl   e 5 litres = ☐ cl   f 25 cl = ☐ ml

g 400 ml = ☐ litres   h 2.5 litres = ☐ ml   i 234 ml = ☐ litres

35 Put these quantities in order of size. Start with the biggest.

a 85 cl, 1250 ml, 16 cl, 0.75 litres, 85 ml, 0.45 litres

b 1200 ml, 0.6 litres, 63 cl, 1.3 litres, 135 cl, 834 ml

36 Stephanie pours out 4 glasses of cola from a 2-litre bottle.

Each glass holds 300 ml. How much cola is left in the bottle?

37 A typical bowl of cereal will have 125 ml of milk.

How many bowls of cereal can a 1-litre carton of milk be used for?

38 Abbey has a pack of 6 bottles of lemonade. Each bottle holds 450 ml.

She uses up all the lemonade by pouring 9 drinks.

How much lemonade is in each drink?

> explanation 7a   explanation 7b

39 A standard ruler often has a metric and an imperial scale.

A standard ruler measures 30 cm, which is approximately 12 inches.

a How many inches are the same as 60 cm?

b How many centimetres are the same as 6 inches?

c How many centimetres are the same as 18 inches?

d Show why 2.5 cm are approximately equal to 1 inch.

40 There are approximately 3 feet in 1 metre.

Mr Jones measures his shed as 6 feet long by 4.5 feet wide.

What is the approximate length and width of the shed in metres?

41 There are approximately 8 km to 5 miles.

a   Daniel's journey to work is 40 km. How many miles is this?

b   Benita's journey to work is 7.5 miles. How many kilometres is this?

42 There are approximately 2.2 lb to 1 kg.

a   A turkey weighs 3.5 kg. How many pounds is this?

b   A bag of potatoes weighs 11 pounds. How many kilograms is this?

43 A gallon is approximately 4.5 litres.

a   How many litres are in 4 gallons?

b   How many gallons are in 45 litres?

c   A litre of petrol costs 98p. How much would a gallon cost?

44 There are approximately 8 km to 5 miles.

Alice and Emma are competing to see who can run the furthest in a week.

Alice runs 3 miles a day for 5 days.

Emma runs 7.5 km three times during the week.

Who run the furthest and by how much?

45 Peter wants to buy a bag of cooking apples.

At the local fruit shop a bag of apples weighing 5.5 lb costs £2.98.

In the supermarket a bag that costs £2.98 weighs 2 kg.

Which shop gives Peter more apples for the money? How much more?

Surface area and volume

- Identifying and drawing nets of cubes and cuboids
- Finding the surface area of cubes and cuboids
- Finding the surface area of a triangular prism
- Calculating the volume of a cuboid
- Calculating the volume of shapes made of cuboids
- Calculating the volume of a prism

Keywords

You should know

explanation 1a   explanation 1b

1 Which of these are *not* possible nets of a cube? Explain why not.

a
	1		
2	3	4	5
	6		

b
5			
1	2	3	4
		6	

c
1	2	3
	4	
	5	
	6	

d
1			2
3	4	5	6

e
	1	
	2	
3	4	
	5	6

f
	1	2
3	4	
	5	6

2 For each of the possible nets in question **1**, work out the face that would be opposite face 1 when folded.

3 The diagram shows a cube.

a How many faces does this cube have?

b What is the area of each face?

c Find the surface area of this cube.

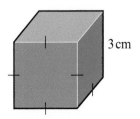
3 cm

---

explanation 2

4 The diagram shows a 4cm by 5cm by 6cm cuboid.

   a The net is made from three different types of rectangles.

     What is the length and width of each of these?

      i the front and back of the cuboid

      ii the base and the top of the cuboid

      iii the sides of the cuboid

   b Draw a net for this 4cm by 5cm by 6cm cuboid.

   c Find the surface area of the cuboid.

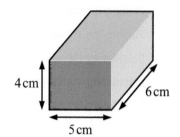

5 Calculate the surface area of each cuboid.

Include the correct units with your answers.

a

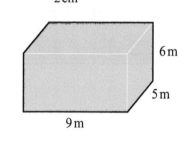

3cm
3cm
10cm

b

8cm
5cm
2cm

c

2mm
10mm
6mm

d

6m
5m
9m

e

6m
4m
15m

f

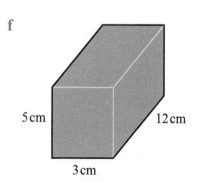

5cm
12cm
3cm

explanation 3a   explanation 3b

*6 Find the volume of each of these 3-D shapes.

a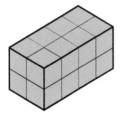

b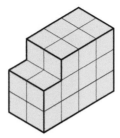

c

7 Here is a cuboid that is 2 cm by 3 cm by 5 cm.

Krishnan wanted to find the volume of the cuboid.

a How can he work out how many cubes are in
the top layer, without counting all the cubes?

b How can he then use the height of the cuboid
to find how many cubes are in the cuboid?

c What is the volume of the cuboid?

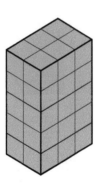

8 Find the volumes of these cuboids.

a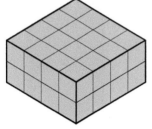

b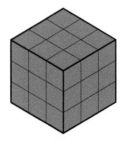

c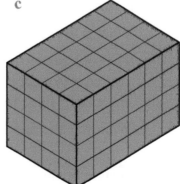

9 Find the volumes of these cuboids.

Include the correct units with your answers.

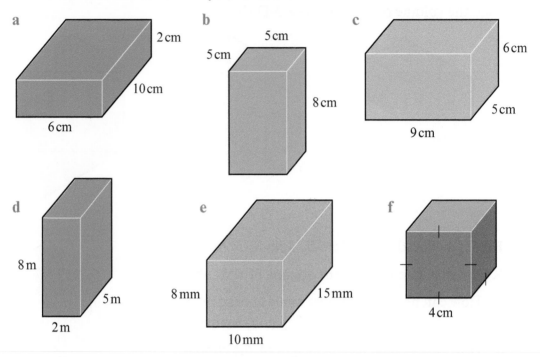

a   2 cm   10 cm   6 cm

b   5 cm   5 cm   8 cm

c   6 cm   5 cm   9 cm

d   8 m   5 m   2 m

e   8 mm   15 mm   10 mm

f   4 cm

10 A box of tea bags measures 15 cm by 13 cm by 8 cm.

A crate can hold 60 boxes of tea. What is the volume of the crate?

11 A carton of orange juice has length 10 cm,
width 6.25 cm and height 16 cm.

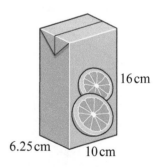

a   What is the volume of the carton?

b   The contents of the carton were
poured into a cube-shaped container
and exactly filled the container.

What was the side length of the container?

16 cm

6.25 cm   10 cm

12 The height of this cuboid is missing
from the diagram.

The volume of the cuboid is 90 cm³.
What is the height of the cuboid?

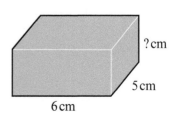

? cm

5 cm

6 cm

13 A cuboid has a square base and a height of 10 cm.

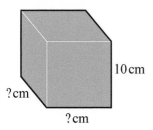

10 cm

? cm

? cm

The volume of the cuboid is 490 cm³. What is the side length of the base?

14 A cube has surface area equal to 150 cm².

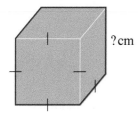

? cm

a   What is the area of each face?

b   What is the side length of the cube?

c   What is the volume of the cube?

15 A cube has volume 27 cm³. What is its surface area?

16 The diagram shows a cuboid and triangular prism, which both have length 6 cm, width 4 cm and perpendicular height 5 cm.

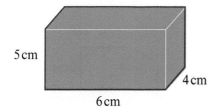

5 cm

4 cm

6 cm

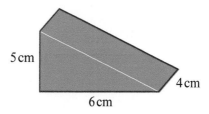

5 cm

4 cm

6 cm

a   How can you find the volume of the triangular prism from the volume of the cuboid?

b   What is the volume of the triangular prism?

explanation 4

17 This 3-D shape can be broken up into two cuboids.

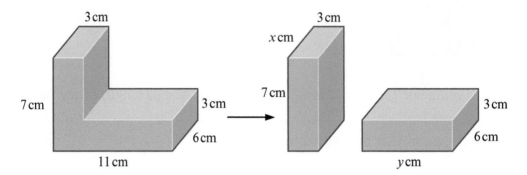

a   Find the missing lengths x and y.

b   Find the volume of the two cuboids.

c   Show that the volume of the original 3-D shape is $270 \, cm^3$.

18 Work out the volume of each of these shapes.

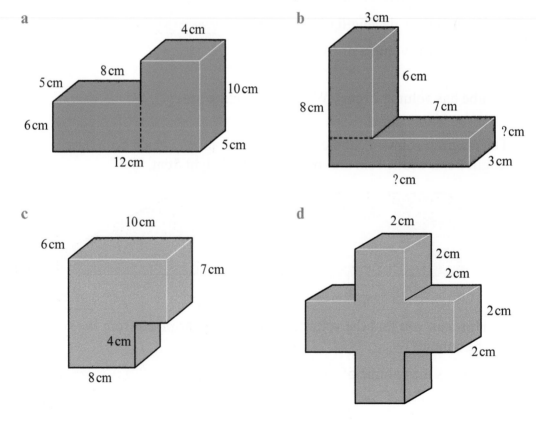

19 The shape from question **17** can be seen as one cuboid with another cuboid removed.

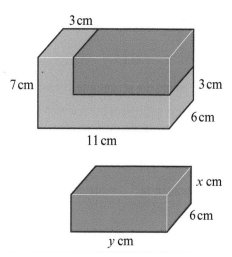

  a Explain why the volume of the large cuboid is 462 cm³.

  b Find the x and y lengths on the smaller cuboid.

  c Find the volume of the smaller cuboid.

  d Show that the volume of the original 3-D shape is 270 cm³.

20 The yellow shape can be seen as one cuboid with the red cuboid removed.

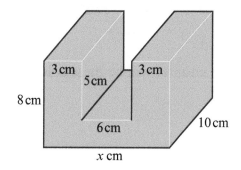
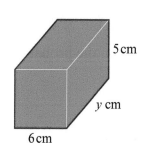

  a Find the missing lengths x and y.

  b Find the volumes of the two cuboids.

  c What is the volume of the original orange shape?

21 Work out the volumes of these shapes.

  a

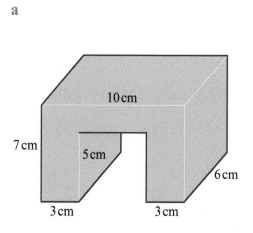

  b

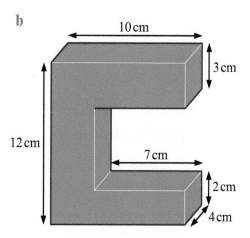

Probability

- Finding the probability of an event not occurring
- Using a diagram to record all the possible outcomes for two successive events

Keywords

You should know

explanation 1a | explanation 1b

1 A bag contains 1 yellow, 4 red and 2 blue counters.

A counter is taken out of the bag at random.

Find, as a fraction, the probability that the counter will be these colours.

a red

b blue

c yellow or blue

d black

2 A fair six-sided spinner has 1 red, 1 yellow, 1 green and 3 blue faces. The spinner is spun once. What is the probability that the spinner will land on these colours?

a yellow

b blue

c purple

3 Jon rolls a fair dice. What is the probability of each of these events?

a a number less than 3

b a multiple of 3

c an even number

d a number greater than 6

4 Amy has 4 red, 3 yellow and 5 blue pencils. She takes a pencil at random. What is the probability that she takes these pencils?

a a yellow pencil

b a blue pencil

c a yellow or a red pencil

d a green pencil

5 A letter is chosen at random from the word EXPERIMENT.

a What is the probability that the letter is X?

b What is the probability that the letter is E?

c What is the probability that the letter is X or E?

6 There are 13 girls and 15 boys in a class. The teacher chooses a pupil at random. What is the probability that she chooses these pupils?

a a girl   b a boy

7 There are 35 cars in a car park. 12 of the cars are silver, 9 are blue, 8 are red and 6 are black.

A car is chosen at random.

a What is the probability that the car is these colours?

   i silver   ii   blue

   iii red   iv   not black

b Add together your answers to parts **i**, **ii** and **iii**.
   Compare this answer with your answer to part **iv**. What do you notice?

(explanation 2a) (explanation 2b)

8 What is the probability that this fair spinner will land on these colours?

a red

b yellow

c not yellow

d either blue or yellow

9   George has twenty toy cars in a box. Nine of the toy cars are black, seven are blue and the rest are red. He takes a car at random from the box.
What is the probability that the car is each of these colours?

   a   black   b   blue   c   not blue

10   The probability that it will snow tomorrow is $\frac{2}{7}$.

   What is the probability that it will not snow tomorrow?

11   Aqbal is going to play snooker with a friend. If the probability that he will win the game is 35%, what is the probability that he will not win the game?

12   Serena is going to the cinema with a friend. The probability that her friend will be late is 0.34. What is the probability that her friend will not be late?

13   A football team play a match. The probability that the team will win is $\frac{5}{11}$ and the probability that the team will draw is $\frac{2}{11}$.
What is the probability that the team will lose the match?

14   Cassie cycles to school. The probability that she will arrive on time is 0.6.
The probability that she will arrive late is 0.1.
What is the probability that she will arrive early?

15   Jake has some pens in his pencil case. The pens are all red, black or blue.
He takes one of these pens at random. The table gives the probabilities that the pen will be red or black. What is the probability that the pen is blue?

Pen colour	Red	Black	Blue
Probability	0.2	0.5	

16   A bag contains only red, yellow, green and blue counters. A counter is taken at random from the bag. The table gives the probabilities that the counter will be red or yellow or green. Work out the probability that the counter will be blue.

Colour	Red	Yellow	Green	Blue
Probability	0.1	0.3	0.2	

17 Jalinda has a box of chocolates.
The chocolates are all milk, plain or white.
She takes a chocolate at random from the box.
The table gives the probabilities of the chocolate
being milk or white.
Work out the probability that the chocolate
will be plain.

Chocolate	Milk	Plain	White
Probability	0.15		0.3

explanation 3a   explanation 3b   explanation 3c

18 Max can choose one main course and one pudding from the menu.

Copy and complete the table to show all the possible combinations that Max could choose.

Main course	Pudding
Curry	Fruit

Menu

Main course
Curry
Fish and chips
Pizza

Pudding
Fruit
Ice cream

19 Sally spins two coins.

a Draw a table to show all the possible ways that the coins could land.

b Use your table to find the probability
of each of these events.

  i Both coins land tails up.

  ii One coin lands heads up and
one coin lands tails up.

20 Ali spins a coin and spins this four-sided spinner.

a Copy and complete the sample space diagram.

		Spinner			
		1	2	3	4
Coin	H	H, 1			
	T			T, 3	

b What is the probability of each event?

  i a tail and an odd number

  ii a head and a number less than 4

21 Barry chooses one letter from box A and
then a letter from box B.
List all the pairs of letters that he could pick.

Box A	Box B
E	C
G	L
B	Z

22 Rory spins two 3-sided spinners.
Some possible outcomes are shown in this sample space diagram.

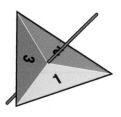

		Spinner 2		
		1	2	3
Spinner 1	1	1, 1		
	2			2, 3
	3		3, 2	

a Copy and complete the diagram.

b What is the total number of possible outcomes?

c What is the probability of getting a 2 and a 3?

d What is the probability of getting two even numbers?

e What is the probability of getting two numbers the same?

23 Jenny is going to colour in three
squares. She only has two colours,
red and green. List all the possible
ways she can colour in the squares.

24 Jeremy rolls two dice.
Some possible outcomes are shown in this sample space diagram.

		Dice 2					
		1	2	3	4	5	6
Dice 1	1	1, 1					
	2						2, 6
	3		3, 2				
	4						
	5					5, 5	
	6			6, 3			

a Copy and complete the diagram.

b What is the total number of possible outcomes?

c What is the probability of getting two odd numbers?

d What is the probability of getting two numbers the same?

e What is the probability of getting at least one six?

f What is the probability of getting no sixes?

25 Malik spins two 3-sided spinners.
He adds the numbers on the spinners together.

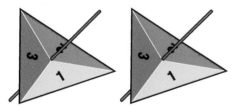

a Draw a sample space diagram to show all the possible outcomes.

b What is the probability of getting an even number?

c What is the probability of getting a score less than 5?

d What is the probability of getting a score greater than 5?

Experiment

- Using an experiment to work out the experimental probability
- Understanding the effect of repeating an experiment many times

Keywords

You should know

explanation 1a   explanation 1b

1 Dennis rolls a biased dice. He records whether or not he gets a 1.

Score	1	Not a 1
Frequency	20	60

    a How many times did Dennis roll the dice?

    b Work out the experimental probability that Dennis will get a 1 the next time he rolls the dice.

2 Katie opens some small boxes of sweets.
    She counts the number of orange sweets in each box.

Number of orange sweets	0	1	2	3	4
Frequency	3	12	10	8	7

    a How many boxes of sweets did Katie open?

    b Work out the experimental probability that the next box of sweets will contain these.

      i 1 orange sweet

      ii 3 orange sweets

      iii less than 3 orange sweets

3 Chaya spins a biased coin. It lands head up 54 times and tail up 36 times.

    a How many times did Chaya spin the coin?

    b Work out the experimental probability that the coin will land head up.

4 Jane carries out a traffic survey.
   She fills in a table showing the total number of each colour of car that passes.

Colour of car	Red	Blue	Silver	White	Green	Black
Frequency	42	60	25	30	5	38

a How many cars did Jane count?

b What colour car is most likely to go past next?

c What colour car is least likely to go past next?

d Work out the experimental probability that the next car to go past will be these colours.

   i white

   ii blue

   iii red

5 Linda puts some red, yellow and blue counters in a bag.
   She takes a counter at random from the bag.
   She records the colour of the counter and then puts the counter back in the bag.

   Linda repeats this experiment 100 times. The table shows her results.

Colour of counter	Red	Yellow	Blue
Frequency	53	14	33

a Which colour counter is there likely to be the most of in the bag?

b Which colour counter is there likely to be the least of in the bag?

c Work out the experimental probability that the next counter to be taken out of the bag will be these colours.

   i yellow

   ii blue

   iii red

explanation 2a explanation 2b

6 You need a coin.

    a Copy the frequency table.

Coin lands	Tally	Frequency
Heads		
Tails		

    b Spin a coin 20 times and record your results in the frequency table.

    c Work out the experimental probability of the coin landing tail up.
       Write your answer as a decimal.

    d Repeat the experiment.

    e Use your results from both experiments to work out probability of the coin
       landing tail up.

    f Compare your answers to parts **c** and **e**. Which is closer to 0.5?
       Is this what you would expect?

7 Work with a partner to carry out an experiment. You are going to work out the
experimental probability of rolling an even number with a dice.

    a One of you should roll the dice 50 times. The other counts how many times
       the dice lands on an even number.

    b How many even numbers did you roll?

    c Work out the experimental probability of rolling an even number.
       Write your answer as a decimal.

    d Repeat parts **a** and **b**. Work out the experimental probability of rolling an
       even number for your second experiment. Write your answer as a decimal.

    e Work out the experimental probability of rolling an even number using your
       results from both experiments. Write your answer as a decimal.

    f Which of your answers to parts **c**, **d** and **e** is closest to 0.5?

    g Your answer to part **e** is likely to be closest to 0.5. Explain why.

    h How could you work out the experimental probability of rolling an even
       number more accurately?

8 Work with a partner.

a Put a total of 10 counters in a bag.
There should be some of three different colours.
Do not let your partner see how many of each colour there are.
Ask your partner to take a counter at random from the bag, record its
colour in a frequency table and then put the counter back.
Repeat this 20 times.

b Work out the experimental probability of taking each colour.
Your partner should use this to estimate how many of each colour counter
there are in the bag.

c Repeat the experiment another 20 times.

d Work out the new experimental probabilities. Your partner should again
estimate how many of each colour counter there are in the bag.

e Repeat this experiment once more and allow your partner one more estimate.

f Empty the bag. Was your partner correct?
Was their final estimate more accurate than their first estimate?

g Change roles and repeat the whole process with you estimating this time.